D1553774

# Frank

# Frank

## The Story of Frances Folsom Cleveland, America's Youngest First Lady

ANNETTE DUNLAP

excelsior editions

State University of New York Press
Albany, New York

Cover photo of Frances Folsom Cleveland in black evening gown, catalog #FFC93.34.a (Large), owned by NJ Division of Parks and Forestry, Grover Cleveland Birthplace

Published by
State University of New York Press, Albany

© 2009 State University of New York

For information, contact State University of New York Press, Albany, NY
www.sunypress.edu

Excelsior Editions is an imprint of State University of New York Press

Production by Diane Ganeles
Marketing by Fran Keneston

**Library of Congress Cataloging-in-Publication Data**

Dunlap, Annette, 1955–
    Frank : the story of Frances Folsom Cleveland, America's youngest first lady / Annette Dunlap.
        p. cm.
    Includes bibliographical references and index.
    ISBN 978-1-4384-2817-8 (hardcover : alk. paper)
    1. Cleveland, Frances Folsom, 1864–1947.    2. Presidents' spouses—United States—Biography.    3. Cleveland, Grover, 1837–1908—Marriage.    I. Title.

    E697.5.C55D86 2009
    973.8'5092—dc22                                          2008054151

10 9 8 7 6 5 4 3 2 1

# Contents

# Illustrations

1. Frances Folsom Cleveland, by C. M. Bell
2. Helena deKay Gilder
3. Frances Cleveland's dog, Kay
4. Emma Folsom Perrine with Ruth and Esther Cleveland
5. Frances Cleveland with Ruth
6. Henry Perrine
7. Marion Cleveland
8. Esther Cleveland
9. Richard Cleveland
10. Francis Grover Cleveland
11. Gray Gables
12. Intermont
13. Frances at Gray Gables with Ruth and Esther
14. Grover Cleveland and Richard Watson Gilder

Photo credits: Grover Cleveland Birthplace Museum

# Note on Spelling

The correspondence quoted in the text is informal writing, and any idiosyncracies of spelling, capitalization, punctuation, and syntax have been retained.

# Acknowledgments

It takes a group of generous and selfless people to support a writer, particularly one who is researching material for a nonfiction work, and I owe thanks to many people.

Special thanks go to Penny Niven, whose writing workshop at Salem College, Winston-Salem, North Carolina, gave me the inspiration to pick this project back up after a ten-year hiatus.

Thanks to Jane Bunker, editor at SUNY Press, who saw merit in the project and gave me a contract.

Thanks to Lewis L. Gould, PhD, professor emeritus of American history at the University of Texas, who answered a stranger's e-mail and directed me to Karen Dunak, researcher par excellence at Indiana University, as well as gave me good advice and recommended readers for this manuscript.

Thanks to Helen Bergamo, head of the archives section at Wells College, for providing research space and collecting the materials on Frances Folsom for me to study.

Thanks to Sharon Farrell, historical interpreter of the Grover Cleveland Birthplace Museum in Caldwell, New Jersey, who gave me an entire day of her time to look at materials and who provided the photographs for this book.

Thanks to the tireless and patient staff in the microfilm section of the Davis Library, at the University of North Carolina–Chapel Hill; Diana in interlibrary loan at the Moore County, NC, library, in Carthage, NC; Mark Schumacher, who pulled out dusty tomes for my use at the University of North Carolina at Greensboro library; the staff of the microfilm section at the University of North Carolina at Asheville library; and the staff in the microfilm section of the D. H. Hill Library at North Carolina State University.

I mentioned Karen Dunak earlier, but let me give her another accolade. All of the Gilder correspondence cited in this biography is the result of her diligent research at the Lilly Library at Indiana University.

Additional thanks to Jim and Jean, friends from my book club who read portions of this manuscript and encouraged me, and to Ralph and Harriett, who did not laugh when I told them what I was doing.

Special thanks to members of the Cleveland family, who allowed me to talk with them.

Thanks to my husband, Bill, who decided that it might be a good idea not to stand in my way once I really got this project started.

Finally, a posthumous appreciation to my mother, Shirley Felman Moritt, who had hoped that she would live long enough to see this book in print.

# 1

# "A little schoolgirl"

May 28, 1886
My dear Sir,
     My marriage with Miss Folsom will take place at the White House on Wednesday (June 2nd) at seven o'clock in the evening.
     I humbly think that I can creditably claim . . . you and Mrs. —— as friends to encourage and sustain us in this new and untried situation.
     May I expect to see you both on this occasion.
                   Yours Sincerely,
                   Grover Cleveland[1]

With a handwritten invitation and a formal announcement from the White House, President Grover Cleveland ended nearly a year of speculation about his marital intentions. The front pages of the nation's major newspapers had covered the story daily from the beginning of May, and gossip in Washington was intense. Cabinet wives pestered their husbands for word of the president's plans, but Cleveland had kept close counsel. Family members and Cleveland's closest confidantes proved their loyalty; they did not reveal the identity of his fiancée.

Washington society had been looking for a bride for the forty-eight-year old bachelor president since he entered the White House in March 1885. A women's reception at the end of March, held by Cleveland's sister, Rose, who was acting as her brother's hostess in the absence of a first lady, provided ideal grist for the rumor mill. The leading candidate for White House bride, from the gossips' perspective, was Miss Van Vechten. Her first name, city of origin, and connection to the Clevelands are lost to history, but a description of her remains. She was tall, commanding, self-possessed, superb, a most thorough and finished woman of the world and society.[2]

Assisting Rose with her duties were Emma Folsom and her daughter, Frances. Mrs. Folsom, a widow, was next in line in Washington society's marital sweepstakes. Described as "a handsome matron, with a gentle, amiable countenance," Emma Folsom exhibited a "protecting, absorbed air" as she presented the visitors to her daughter, and "intently watched every motion of the young girl and encouraged her in the ordeal."[3]

In contrast, Frances Folsom was portrayed as innocent and naive. Her age was given as nineteen (she was actually a few months shy of her twenty-first birthday), and some reporters characterized her as timid, restrained, and unaccustomed to being in society.[4] The *Washington Post* was somewhat more charitable, describing her as the "fresh and charming schoolgirl, with a rich color in her cheeks and a rather shy, constrained manner."[5] "Miss Folsom," it continued, "stood next to her mother in a simple dress of white nun's veiling and surah, with some cascades of lace on waist and skirt, and her corsage bouquet of Jacqueminot roses matched the excited color that flamed in her cheeks."[6]

Frank, as she was known to her family, had both her supporters and her detractors at the reception. Mrs. Daniel S. Lamont, the wife of President Cleveland's personal secretary, commented about Frank to another woman at the reception, "Isn't she the loveliest, the sweetest little beauty you every saw?"

Mrs. Lamont's companion, however, thought otherwise. "Charming, charming. How perfectly ridiculous it is to talk of the President marrying that child. The mother is even a trifle young for a man of his years and seriousness, and he will never marry while he lives in this house, I know. That sort of thing is not in his line and not in his mind, now that he has the duties of this great office on his shoulders."[7]

But Cleveland very much had "that sort of thing" in his mind, as he admitted to a friend many years later. "Poor girl, I often say to my wife. You never had any courting like other girls. It is true I did say some things to her one night, when we were walking in the East Room, when she was here visiting my sister."[8]

After the reception, Frank returned to Wells College, and was one of five women in the class that graduated on June 20, 1885. The commencement program listed her as Frank Folsom, of Buffalo, New York. Although she had no special honors at Wells, she had become a favorite of the faculty, was a leader among her classmates, and had established friendships with other women that provided her with an anchor for what became a very public life. Cleveland did not attend the ceremonies, but he sent hampers of flowers and ivy, which Frank and her classmates planted along the side of the college's Morgan Hall.

In midsummer, Cleveland proposed marriage in a letter written to Frank while she was visiting family in Scranton. "Would you put your life in my hands?" he asked, and she answered "Yes." The couple and their families agreed to keep the engagement a secret, and no firm wedding date was set.

Frank's cousin, Benjamin Folsom, wrote Cleveland in October that he would like to accompany Frank and her mother on a trip to Europe. In the spring, when news of the engagement began to appear in the press, people speculated that Cleveland had paid for the trip so that Frank could purchase a trousseau and learn the ways of the European courts.

Frank's grandfather, Colonel John B. Folsom, responded strongly when asked if Cleveland had paid Frank's expenses. "That is an infamous lie, sir," Folsom retorted.

"Grover Cleveland would not offer to do it knowing that it would be distasteful to us. . . . I told Frankie she should buy her trousseau, as the newspapers call it, in Paris, if she wanted to, and I told her to draw on me to pay for it. I want her to ask me for money. The only condition I imposed was that she should get as fine a costume as possible."[9]

If the family thought there was anything inappropriate about the relationship between the forty-eight-year-old Cleveland and the twenty-one-year-old Frank, it was carefully concealed. Her cousin, Ben Folsom, a longtime friend of Cleveland's, regarded him with appropriate deference and respect as Frank's fiancé. Colonel Folsom, likewise, did not question the propriety of the relationship. Emma Folsom, who would have had the support of her mother, brother, and sisters had she objected, evidently approved the match. "[Frank] made a hero of him before she was out of short dresses; and [she] looks at him through the glamour of love's young dream," Emma commented approvingly about the relationship.[10]

On Cleveland's side, his letters to his sisters Susan C. Yeomans and Mary C. Hoyt suggest that they accepted their brother's engagement to a woman who was certainly young enough to be one of their daughters. Rose Cleveland, commenting on the event of the wedding, hinted to the press that her new sister-in-law was more than just another pretty face.

Kate Willard, Frank's former roommate at Wells, on the other hand, made several attempts to discourage Frank from marrying Cleveland. Kate had left Wells in late 1884 or early 1885 to join her mother, Mary Bannister Willard, in Germany. Mary oversaw the Women's Christian Temperance Union's European activities and had started the American School for Girls, in Berlin. Kate traveled to Europe to study vocal music.

Kate's letters to Frank over the years reflect Kate's own reluctance to marry, and she was jealous of Frank and Cleveland's relationship. Even so, the letter written immediately after the two friends parted company after visiting together in Italy demonstrates a genuine concern on Kate's part for her friend's happiness. Kate wrote Frank:

> I think I shall tell you what I could scarcely help from writing on the third of March. . . . On that day I should have begged you wildly never, never to marry Mr. Cleveland, and doubtless give you very good reasons for hindering you. . . .
>
> I am not disappointed that this seems to you to be the right thing: only disappointed because I had thought of another life and love for you. I don't know *what*, only not this, and I am slow to see the best thing. I believe you know I want you to be happy, and I want you to make other people happy. I am only afraid I have not chosen *your* way of doing this.
>
> I trust you, Frank, if I know you "love the best thing" more than I do, I think, inasmuch as you do them often, and so I am bound to believe you are doing what

seemed the best thing . . . but I believe you think of that side, too, from your saying in your note to me that [you] had found your "mission."[11]

Cleveland's doubts were of a wholly different nature. In his letters to Frank, he often reminded her that his public office would greatly intrude into their private relationship. If Frank understood the extent to which Cleveland's devotion to duty, coupled with the expectations of Washington society, would infringe on their marriage, she did not waver in her commitment.

Cleveland's other concern was whether he would be able to "make" Frank into a sensible woman. His letter to his sister, Mary, suggests that he wanted to have control over Frank:

> It has occurred to me that it would be nice to have the little room adjoining mine which William [Cleveland's valet] occupies fixed up for a dressing room, etc., for Frank, or a place where she could sit and stay during the day. . . .
>
> I have my heart set upon making Frank a sensible, domestic American wife, and I would be pleased not to hear her spoken of as "The First Lady of the Land" or "The Mistress of the White House." I want her to be happy and to possess all she can reasonably desire, but I should feel very much afflicted if she lets many notions in her head. But I think she is pretty levelheaded. . . .[12]

Cleveland eventually decided that Frank was not a petulant schoolgirl. When the couple visited St. Paul, Minnesota, during their western and southern tour in 1887, Cleveland addressed a group by noting that his wife had once lived there. "I thank you that you did not spoil my wife," he told the group.

Cleveland's mind might have been set at ease had he read Kate's letter to Frank, written a month earlier. "I don't think you are weak, Frank," Willard wrote her friend. "I think you have ruled and controlled yourself during the time I've known you as thoroughly as anyone I know. And as for evenness of action day in and day out, you have been more [unintelligible word] than any friend I have ever had. . . ."[13]

By April, the press had wind of rumors that the president was engaged. Miss Van Vechten had long since disappeared from the scene. Now the press speculated as to whether Cleveland's fiancée was the young "Frankie" or her mother, the older, more mature, Mrs. Emma Folsom.

Washington watchers speculated that a marriage was in the offing when Rose Cleveland did not join her brother after Easter for the spring 1886 social season. By early May, newspapers were writing that the rumors of pending presidential nuptials were true. Just confirming the suspicions was not enough to satisfy the curious reporters. They wanted to know the who, what, and when of the details, and expressed dismay at being left in the dark.

Cleveland, for the most part, kept his counsel, although he was quoted as telling some friends during an afternoon's carriage ride, "I don't see why the papers keep marrying me to old ladies all the while. I wonder why they don't say I am engaged to marry her daughter."[14]

Evidence of Cleveland's choice of bride could be found in Frank's hometown, Buffalo. Sometime during her stay in Europe, Frank wrote Cora Townsend to announce her engagement. Mrs. Townsend was most likely the mother of Frank's first fiancé, Charles. As was the family's custom, Cora began reading Frank's letter aloud to the family at the breakfast table. It was not until she reached the end of the note that she read the request to keep the matter a secret. By then, it was obviously too late. The word was out, but the press still doubted the truth of the information.

As late as May 26, just a week before the wedding took place, the hometown papers "reported that the engagement of President Cleveland and Miss Folsom, of Buffalo, probably received less credence in this city than anywhere else in the country."[15]

Frances herself was reported to have denied her engagement to Miss Granger, a close friend who visited Frances in Paris. Two days before the official announcement was made on May 30, the *New York Times* wrote, "[T]he marriage between Mrs. or Miss Folsom is still uncertain. The President's wish to keep the matter private only incites greater interest in the feminine minds of this country."[16]

Reporters, hungry for even the slightest tidbit of information about the identity of the president's bride, quickly realized that Daniel Lamont might be the key to an answer. He had been dispatched by

Cleveland to New York to assist the Folsoms with their return from Europe. He met their boat when it docked during the night of May 27, 1886, helped them get through customs, and got them situated in their accommodations at Gilsey House, in Manhattan.

Lamont carried out his activities undetected. His silence as he went about his tasks prompted the *Times* to complain, "Lamont would not confirm whom the President is to marry. The steamship company denies that the Folsoms are on the City of Chicago," which was another steamship in its line. Sarcastically, the paper added, "[Lamont] will depart as mysteriously as he came, and anyone who secures the slightest information from him concerning his visit to New York will receive a Government pension of $500 a week."[17]

Part of the reason for the delay was that the wedding date itself had not been confirmed prior to Frances's European tour. A June date had been discussed, and there were tentative plans for Frances and the president to marry at Colonel Folsom's farm. Folsom's death, on May 22, while Frances, her mother, and cousin were en route from London eliminated that possibility.

Frank did not learn of her grandfather's death until she reached New York. At that point, Cleveland was able to communicate with Frank, and she apparently suggested the June 2 date. The wedding would now be at the White House. In consideration of her grandfather's very recent death, the occasion would be a quiet, private affair.

In retrospect, the absorption of the press with the identity of Cleveland's bride is humorous. Cleveland secretly courted Frank in plain sight, but no one caught on. Like all other men who corresponded with Wells students, Cleveland had obtained family permission to send Frank letters. Helen Fairchild Smith scrutinized the mails and the male visitors who called upon "her girls." Governor Grover Cleveland was no exception. Students noted his portrait in Frank's room, but she always referred to him as "Uncle Cleve" or "the Governor."

Frank's travels with Cleveland around New York, after he became governor, were not considered unusual. And her regular receipt of flowers from the governor's mansion, and then the White House, did not tip off any students that a romance was developing.

Cleveland's fervent wish was to keep the press as far away as possible. In a letter to his sister, Mary, dated March 21, 1886, Cleveland wrote:

I expect to be married pretty early in June—very soon after Frank returns. I think the quicker it can be done the better and she seems to think so too. You know she can hardly be said to have a home, and if the event was delayed long after her return the talk and gossip which would certainly be stirred up could not fail to be very embarrassing to her. I find it very hard to settle the question as to the manner in which the thing should be conducted. . . .

I want my marriage to be a quiet one and am determined that the American Sovereigns shall not interfere with a thing so purely personal to me. And yet I don't want to be churlish and mean or peculiar for the sake of being peculiar. But if the example of the President is worth anything I want it in this matter to be in the direction of sense and proper decency. . . .[18]

The "American Sovereigns" were very intent on interfering. Before Frank's accommodations were finally confirmed, reporters combed the city to learn where she and her family were staying. Women asked the clerks in their respective hotels if the president's bride-to-be was staying there. "The attachés of all the hotels were besieged from morning until night with inquiries and were much wearied with their task," the *New York Times* reported. One reporter said, "I have rarely seen such public interest. It is simply marvelous."[19]

Neither Cleveland, Lamont, nor the Folsoms found the hounding "simply marvelous." To combat the public clamor for a glimpse of Frances, her cousin released a statement saying that Miss Folsom would not respond to cards left at the front desk. She only wanted to see a few intimate friends; they already knew her room number, and would reach her rooms on their own.

President Cleveland left Washington by train on Sunday, May 30, to attend the Decoration Day ceremonies the following day in New York. The press and public tracked his every movement. Interest in the president's romantic life intensified. Word of Cleveland's departure time from the train station in Washington, where he traveled in a special car attached to a regularly scheduled train of the Pennsylvania Railroad, was telegraphed to New York, and a party of the curious and of well-wishers awaited his arrival there.

The veterans of the Grand Army of the Republic played second fiddle to the future Mrs. Grover Cleveland at New York's Decoration Day Parade, on May 31, 1886. Thousands of pairs of eyes were occupied more with the details of her figure than with the contemplation of the parade.[20] Joined by Benjamin Folsom and Mrs. Lamont, Frank and her party traveled by carriage to the Fifth Avenue Hotel, where she watched the parade from an upstairs window. The bands recognized her, and as President Cleveland passed underneath the window, struck up the tune, "He's Going to Marry Yum-Yum," from the then-popular Gilbert & Sullivan musical, *The Mikado*.

As Cleveland passed underneath Frank's window, he tipped his hat in acknowledgment, and she responded by a wave of her handkerchief. The crowd roared its appreciation of the gestures. After all his efforts to keep his romantic affairs private, Cleveland showed visible appreciation for the public's enthusiastic approval.

Frank and her mother arrived by train from New York at six o'clock on the morning of the wedding, Wednesday, June 2, 1886. Cleveland and Rose were there to greet Frank; her mother, Emma; and her cousin, Ben. They breakfasted together, and afterward Cleveland returned to work as if nothing out of the ordinary were scheduled for his day.

Reporters staked out the White House and observed the day's activities, looking for more information about the type of wedding the president would have that evening. The wedding cake arrived by a limited express train from New York, and the individual boxes, containing the cake's multilayer tiers, were removed under the watchful eyes of the baggage men. A carriage transported the cake boxes from the station to the White House.

Representatives of the press were allowed a brief glimpse of the wedding decorations at five o'clock that afternoon, when the White House attendants opened the doors to the parlors.

At six, area church bells tolled in anticipatory celebration of the wedding. As the time for the ceremony neared, people gathered in front of the White House. The papers numbered the crowds in the hundreds.

The presidential mansion, in 1886, was unguarded, and since it was considered a possession of the people of the United States, it was publicly accessible. The *New York Times* reported, "It was a jolly, good-natured gathering and thoroughly democratic. There was the ragged street arab and the well-to-do merchant and his wife, the slipshod colored girl and the lady in silk attire, the rough laborer, bricklayer or hodcarrier and the neatly-dressed clerk from the stores. The gates were left wide open. Everybody could come in and everybody who was so disposed entered the wide portals and passed up the wide asphalt drive to the very portals of the White House itself."[21]

The crowd stood by and watched as the wedding guests arrived in their carriages. The total wedding party numbered under thirty, consisting of the president's immediate family; Benjamin and Mrs. Folsom and other members of Frank's family; members of Cleveland's cabinet and their wives; and selected friends of both sides from Buffalo, including Julia Severance.

Rose Cleveland oversaw the wedding preparations for her brother and his bride. The White House's extensive greenhouses furnished the flowers for wedding decorations. The Blue Room had been completely transformed. "The crystal chandelier poured a flood of mellow radiance upon the scene, and the colors of the massive banks of scarlet begonias and royal Jacqueminot roses mingling with the blue and silver tints of the frescoed walls and ceiling gave a warm and glowing tone to the whole brilliant interior."[22]

The letters *C* and *F* were interwoven in moss and white roses through the dark red Jacqueminot bouquets on the mantel. Tall tropical plants concealed the view of the room from the outside. The fireplace was filled with flowers that represented the colors of a blaze.

The East Room was similarly decorated with groups of palms, ferns, azaleas, and hydrangeas in the window spaces. Garlands of roses trimmed the four columns that supported the ceiling, and banks of orchids, lilies, and roses were arranged along the four large mantels in the room.

At exactly seven o'clock, the crowd heard the strains of the "Wedding Chorus" from *Lohengrin* performed by the Marine Band, under the direction of John Philip Sousa, and whispered to one another that the service had begun. A presidential salute was fired from the southern end of the city, and church bells pealed in celebration.

The president descended the western staircase, with Frank on his arm. With a nod, he signaled that the music was to stop. The two stood together in the center of the room, facing Dr. Byron Sunderland, the pastor of Washington's First Presbyterian Church, and Reverend William Cleveland, the president's brother. The guests stood in a semicircle behind the couple.

The physical contrast between the two was captured by an artist's rendering of the ceremony. Cleveland, a stout man of 250 pounds, looks distinctly middle-aged next to his young bride. His heavy, dark mustache was carefully trimmed, but nothing could disguise his very noticeable double chin, or his receding hairline. Cecil Spring-Rice, who joined the British Consulate in 1887, wrote to a friend in England, "The President is 5 feet high and 4 feet wide: he has no neck and six chins."[23] The philosopher and historian Henry Adams observed to his wife, "We must admit that, like Abraham Lincoln, the Lord made a mighty common-looking man in him."[24]

On the other hand, the press immediately characterized Frances as a beauty. She was a half a head shorter than Cleveland, shapely, and considered "full-bosomed." Her dark, luxurious hair was piled atop her head in the typical fashion of the day. She had expressive blue-gray eyes and a youthful, fresh complexion.

At Sunderland's direction, the two joined their right hands to signify their willingness to marry. Cleveland had changed Frank's vows, substituting the word "keep" for "obey." The gold ring that he placed on her finger was inscribed "June 2, 1886." Cleveland and his bride did not kiss at the end of the ceremony. Mrs. Folsom was the first to offer her congratulations, and the new Mrs. Cleveland kissed each of the women in attendance. "The gentlemen were not so favored," the *Post* noted.[25]

Cleveland, who typically showed little interest in his personal appearance, had dressed with unusual care for the ceremony. "[He] wore a smoothly fitting dress suit of black broadcloth, patent leather shoes, white kid gloves, wearing the left and carrying the right one. His low cut vest displayed an expanse of shirt bosom in which were three flat white studs. A white lawn tie encircled his standing collar."[26]

Frances's wedding gown was made of ivory satin, "simply garnished on the high corsage with India muslin crossed in Grecian folds and carried in exquisite falls of simplicity over the petticoat." Orange blossoms were woven throughout her five-yard-long veil of tulle in the shape of a crown. The veil "completely enveloped her, falling to the edge of the petticoat in front and extending the entire length of her full court train." Frances's only jewelry was her diamond-and-sapphire engagement ring.[27]

The newlyweds led the way to the family dining room for an informal supper. Cleveland and his new bride stood in front of the now-assembled, huge wedding cake. Frances cut the cake with a pearl-handled knife, signaling the beginning of the toasts and the meal.

Rose Cleveland, who had been especially attentive to her brother's bride, handed Frank a glass of sparkling water with which she could drink the toasts to her marriage. Like Frank, Rose had taken a temperance vow. Unlike her predecessor, "Lemonade Lucy" Hayes, the new Mrs. Cleveland did not deny others their enjoyment of alcoholic beverages.

The guests were favored with satin bags and boxes of bonbons in every conceivable variety and shape. The newlyweds had found time prior to the ceremony to each sign a small card that was tied to a small box, handpainted with a spray of flowers that contained a piece of the wedding cake.

Cleveland and his bride did not linger in the dining room, but left to change for their honeymoon. Cleveland emerged first, wearing a black suit and Prince Albert frock. Frank's traveling outfit was a deep-gray suit and matching large gray hat lined with velvet and trimmed with picot ribbons and ostrich feathers.

They said their good-byes in the main corridor of the White House and left the White House via the southern balcony. Rice, old slippers, and wishes of "Godspeed" followed them as they drove away in an enclosed carriage.

Cleveland thought that he had outwitted the newspaper reporters that lined the streets hoping to catch a glimpse of the newlyweds. The carriage followed a less heavily traveled road, and brought the Clevelands to a side track away from the main depot of the Baltimore and Ohio Railroad. There a train of two cars and an engine waited to take the couple to Deer Park, Maryland.

But as Cleveland learned the next day, he was the one who was outwitted. The reporters hired a train to follow the couple, and newspapermen hid in the trees around the resort hoping to learn whatever they could about the lives of the newly married couple.

# 2

# "A peculiarly happy disposition"

Frances Clara Folsom's life changed irrevocably two days after her eleventh birthday. On the night of July 23, 1875, her father, Oscar Folsom, died in a carriage accident. He was driving his buggy in Buffalo, and approached an intersection where the back end of a cart extended into the road. The angle of the approach and the early evening dusk concealed the wagon until the last minute. When Folsom attempted to avoid hitting the cart, he was thrown from the buggy. The fall fractured his skull, and his startled horse took off at a run, causing the rear wheel of Folsom's rig to run over him. The accident occurred shortly before eight in the evening. Folsom was declared dead at midnight.[1]

The adjectives used to describe Folsom were remarkably similar to those that would be used to describe his daughter ten years later: "a peculiarly happy disposition and unchanging kindliness."[2] Folsom also had a passion for horse racing and gambling, and his generosity often hurt his family's well-being. His finances, at his death, were "much mixed up."[3]

Folsom presumably had a $5,000 life insurance policy, with Cleveland named as executor of the proceeds. Folsom's debts totaled $16,380.49, and he had a mere $2,166.47 in receivables. An IOU was found in Folsom's office for a debt of $1,040 owed to his former law partner, Grover Cleveland.[4]

Grover Cleveland was one of the pallbearer's at his friend's funeral. The two had become acquainted shortly after Folsom's arrival in Buffalo, New York, in 1861, where he had moved to practice law. The burgeoning of the railroad industry afforded Cleveland and Folsom the chance to build a legal practice, and Cleveland, the more industrious of the two, was more successful. Folsom paid little attention to detail, and during the short time that the two were law partners, Folsom so frequently asked Cleveland about points of the law that Cleveland eventually retorted in exasperation, "Go look it up yourself."

Following Folsom's death, the court named Grover Cleveland as the administrator of Folsom's estate. In an unusual move, it did not assign Frances to Cleveland as his ward. It was customary at the time for a man to be named as the guardian of a minor child, even if the child's mother were alive and competent, and Cleveland may have been asked to assume that role. If so, he apparently declined the request, possibly because he already had "tender feelings" for his late friend's daughter. Cleveland's sister, Susan, once asked her bachelor brother, on the occasion of a family wedding, if he ever intended to marry. "Yes," he replied. "I am waiting for my sweetheart to grow up."[5]

Emma needed Cleveland's fiscal conservatism and sound legal judgment to protect what few assets she had, and she could not have found a better administrator than Grover Cleveland. People admired his integrity, and he represented many of the railroads and businesses in western New York that needed the services of a financially astute attorney. Chauncey Depew, president of the New York Central Railroad, wrote in his memoirs, "I knew Mr. Cleveland, and as evidence of my appreciation for his ability, when the office of general counsel of the New York Central Railroad at Buffalo became vacant, I offered it to him."[6]

Grover Cleveland and Oscar Folsom had some notable similarities. Both were men of medium height and significant girth. They were also alike in their shared enjoyment of good food, hunting and fishing, and the conviviality of other men. Beyond that, they could not have been more different.

Folsom's family had a long and rich history in upstate New York. Oscar Folsom's father, Colonel Folsom, had served in both a military and advisory capacity to several of New York's early governors, including William H. Seward. The Folsoms had been active leaders in the Baptist Church, and they were one of the founding families of the University of Rochester, which opened in 1850. Folsom graduated from the university in 1859.

By contrast, Cleveland was an impoverished child of the manse. His father, an itinerant Presbyterian clergyman who was never able to hold on to a church position for any length of time, died suddenly after assuming the pastorate of a church in Holland Patent, New York. The fifth of nine children, Cleveland abandoned plans to attend college, and after working for a year as a teacher at the New York Institute for the Blind, he traveled to Buffalo to work with his uncle, Lewis Allen. With the money Cleveland earned from helping his uncle compile *Allen's American Shorthorn Herd Book*, Cleveland paid for the right to read law and clerk with the Buffalo firm Rogers, Bowen and Rogers.

Cleveland was already a member of the bar when Folsom moved to Buffalo. Folsom was engaged to Emma Harmon, and he mentioned Cleveland in an 1862 letter to her.

"My own Em," Folsom wrote, recounting a visit to her sister, Helen, who lived in Buffalo. "I walked up to the cottage with Helen after the 'show' and was also up to see her Friday evening accompanied by my friend Grover Cleveland. He is very much pleased with her and thinks he would like to see her sister, but this he of course must not be permitted to do. He is such a pleasant fellow that I should get jealous of him very soon."[7]

Emma and Folsom married in 1863, and their first child, Frances Clara, was born on July 21, 1864. She was immediately known as "Frank," a popular diminutive for "Frances" and the name that her namesake, Aunt Frank, was known by. Cleveland bought the Folsoms' new baby her first carriage, and he became a regular visitor in the Folsom home. As young Frank grew, she called her parents' close friend "Uncle Cleve."

Cleveland's assumption of the role of administrator of Folsom's estate was not the first time that Cleveland had rescued his friend, or protected his friend's family. In 1873, the Folsoms moved back to Folsomdale to help Oscar Folsom's sister-in-law care for her four children following his brother's death in February. Folsom maintained his law office in Buffalo, and the travel created enough distance from his wife and daughter for Folsom to get involved, without suspicion, with a Buffalo widow by the name of Maria Halpin. She gave birth to an illegitimate son in September 1874, and named the boy Oscar Folsom Cleveland.

Grover Cleveland assumed the paternal responsibility for the infant. Many believed that he did so because he was the only unmarried man with whom Halpin had been intimate, and he wanted to protect the other, married attorneys who had slept with her, especially his friend, Oscar Folsom, most likely the baby's father.

At the time, the birth of an illegitimate child to an indigent woman was sufficiently commonplace in Buffalo's rough-and-tumble Canal District not to draw attention. When Halpin's alcoholism left her incapable of caring for her son, Cleveland stepped in and arranged for the child to be adopted. The matter was handled unobtrusively at the time, but it would have far-reaching implications just a short decade later.

Cleveland's steady hand at the helm of Emma's finances could not provide equally steady comfort for her in her grief. In the two years following her husband's death, Emma looked for a place to settle down where both she and Frank could be happy.

Staying at the Folsom farm was no longer an option. Although Colonel Folsom continued to provide for "little Frank's" financial needs, Emma was uncomfortable staying in a home where her father-in-law had lost his wife and all three of his adult children within a two-year period.

Emma moved to St. Paul, Minnesota, to stay with her sister, but the home was fraught with tensions as her sister, Nellie, struggled to salvage a marriage that was deteriorating. Emma returned to Medina, New York, to live with her mother, but Emma's brother, Milton, had moved to Jackson, Michigan, the previous year and, having become successfully established, invited his mother and sister to join him. Ruth Harmon sold her farm and home to join her son.

Emma and Frank returned to Buffalo, first living in a series of boardinghouses and finally settling in a rented house on Pearl Street. They spent their summers with the surviving Folsoms in Folsomdale, and joined the Harmons in Michigan for Christmas. The pattern continued until Frank's marriage in 1886.

Upon her return to Buffalo, Frank attended Central High School, where she did not especially stand out from the other students. Those who remembered her at the time of her wedding described her as a good and conscientious student, who learned rapidly and had a good memory. According to one teacher, Frank "always put a little of herself into her recitations."[8] The name "Frank" landed her on the boys' lists at Central so often that she started going by the name "Frank Clara."

While still at Central, Frank was courted by Charles Townsend, of Buffalo, who was attending the seminary in Auburn, New York. He proposed marriage, and she accepted the offer. Within a few months, however, Frank returned the ring with a letter to the young man. She indicated that they would be better off as just friends.

The engagement to a seminary student was a natural fit for Frank's religious commitment and her warm personality. She joined the Presbyterian Church at the age of fourteen, and throughout her life, her actions were governed by adherence to the teachings and the work of the church. She honored the temperance vow she made as a teenager until old age, when a physician recommended a morning shot of brandy to treat her heart disease. Frank was a disciplined Sabbatarian, who believed that no work or entertainment should take place on Sunday. She was a firm believer in the mission work of the church, and served for many years on the board of the Home Mission Society of the Presbyterian Church.

Cleveland, also raised in a Presbyterian home, had seen the dark side of serving a church. Failure and poverty had characterized his father's ministerial career. The family of two adults and nine children lacked sufficient money to meet expenses. The scars left from life in the manse were evident in Cleveland's abandonment of most of the religious practices he had known as a youth. Cleveland, as financial advisor and close family friend, could naturally have suggested to Emma, and maybe even to Frank herself, that she think carefully about becoming committed to a marriage in which she would serve as a minister's wife.

Frank dropped out of Central High School in October 1881. In January 1882, she enrolled in Wells College, in Aurora, New York, with the equivalent of sophomore standing. Cleveland, who had been elected mayor of Buffalo in November 1881, used his influence to obtain a certificate of high school graduation for Frank. He also arranged for her to enter Wells.

Wells College is located on Cayuga Lake, in New York's Finger Lakes region. The picturesque campus is nestled in the area's low-lying hills, facing the waterfront. Cornell University, in Ithaca, founded at the same time as Wells, lay thirty miles away, and both campuses were near the socially activist communities of Auburn and Seneca Falls.

Henry Wells, the founder of the Wells Fargo and American Express companies, built the college as part of his estate. "Henry Wells had long had the idea of founding a college for women in his mind. In 1850 he came to make his home in the village of Aurora, on the shores of Cayuga Lake," writes the Wells College historian Jane Marsh Dieckmann. Wells inaugurated Wells Seminary on July 23, 1868, following the passage of an "act of incorporation for Wells Seminary for the higher education of young women" on March 28, 1868, by the New York State Legislature.[9]

The school was founded with a prestigious list of influential men from the region as trustees. They included Frederick W. Seward of Auburn, a son of William H. Seward and a law partner of former president Millard Fillmore; Fillmore's postmaster general, Nathan K. Hall; and Charles J. Folger, who became secretary of the treasury under Chester Arthur in 1881.[10]

Wells was one of several female colleges and seminaries that had cropped up in the region during the 1870s. Cleveland and Emma may have learned of Wells from William G. Fargo, a former mayor of Buffalo, and Wells's partner in the express business. Another possible reason for Frank's selection of Wells was its strong affiliation with the Presbyterian Church. Wells women had pews assigned to them in the Aurora Presbyterian church, to be occupied on Sundays.[11]

The education provided at Wells College was little influenced by the rich abolitionist heritage of upstate New York or by the women's rights movement headquartered a mere fifteen miles down the road, in Seneca Falls. The college offered the very type of "finishing" that Emma had in mind for her daughter, and of which Cleveland approved.

The woman primarily responsible for the students' social and intellectual education was Helen Fairchild Smith, who was hired in August 1876 as the school's lady principal. She was described by the *Rochester Democrat* as a "lady of superior education and culture, admirably suited for teaching." Her father had been president of Wesleyan University and a mathematics professor at the U.S. Naval Academy. Smith was a dominant figure at the college for thirty years, and throughout her long tenure she was known for high moral standards, a wide interest in everything human, and a personality that many found charming.[12]

If there was any one woman who single-handedly prepared Frances Clara Folsom to become the nation's first lady, it was Helen Fairchild Smith. Colonel Morgan, a trustee of and generous benefactor to the college, reportedly once said of her, "to know Miss Smith was a liberal education in itself." Her standards of behavior were equally high and, with the oft-repeated words "Never forget you are a Wells girl," she taught the young women to behave properly—politely, graciously, honestly. As Jean S. Davis, professor emerita of Wells, put it much later, Dean Smith "considered it her duty to train all her charges for the formal life of ladies of that period. Everyone dressed for dinner—a custom which continued in Aurora for college and village until the Great Depression. . . ."[13]

Smith was very short and stood very erect. She was always correct and dignified, and many felt that she looked something like Queen Victoria. Already forty years old when she came, she must have seemed antiquated to the students. Her relationship to them was maternal, with all that meant in their training and discipline. Many remembered her wise influence, her reading to them, her kindly affection. She dealt with them skillfully—she kept a handwritten book of their birthdays, listed alphabetically. There was never any question, however, who was in charge of the college family.[14]

Whatever Frank had been missing at Buffalo's Central School, she found at Wells College. She immediately became immersed in the school's social and cultural activities, and quickly assumed a leadership role. One recollection of Frank entering the college dining hall described her as follows: "The leader was a girl of eighteen, perhaps, but her tall, fine figure, her manner of dress, and her air of composure made her appear older than her companions. She was warmly greeted by the teachers as 'Frank,' and the new girls . . . captivated by her grace and beauty, put down their knives and forks to look after her. . . ."[15]

Wells attracted girls from other parts of the country, and Frank formed friendships with several of her classmates that lasted until her death. Julia Walworth Severance, who was born in Cleveland, Ohio, eventually became a member of the Wells College Board of Trustees, and served with Frank in that capacity. Minnie Rachel Scott, also from

Ohio, maintained her friendship with Frank even after she became first lady, and served for a time as Frank's personal secretary. Virginia Kingsford, from Oswego, New York, was another friend.

In the fall of 1882, Katherine Willard, who was two years younger than Frank, became Frank's roommate. As a young girl, Kate had also lost her father. Oliver Willard had been trained as a minister, but his temperament and drinking problem had made it difficult for him to hold down pastoral employment for any length of time. Instead, Willard became the publisher and editor of the *Chicago Post*, but the newspaper was in financial straits upon his death. His widow, Mary Bannister Willard, could not resurrect the troubled company, and its demise left her and her children impoverished. Kate's aunt, Frances Willard, was the founder and president of the Women's Christian Temperance Union. The organization was run completely by females, who, without any significant male involvement, raised money, traveled the world, spoke on behalf of downtrodden women and children, and ministered to the needs of alcoholics on America's skid rows.

Kate never finished at Wells. In 1885, she joined her mother in Germany to assist with the international work of the WCTU and to study voice. Katherine, who lived in a world of successful women, had no desire to marry, and hers was the lone voice discouraging Frank from marriage to Cleveland. She and Frank remained friends, and Frank eventually introduced Kate to William Baldwin, an undersecretary of state in the second Cleveland administration, whom Kate ultimately married.

Frank became a favorite of the faculty and excelled in her studies. The 1882–83 grade book shows that her grade point averages were consistently in the mid-90s, with a strong performance in English, vocal music, and history.

While Frank blossomed within the Wells community, Cleveland's political career grew as well. His willingness to tackle the seemingly intransigent issues of civil service reform and the role of political bosses won him the attention of New York's Democratic Party. In 1882, Cleveland was nominated for governor. In spite of the state's strong Republican Party, he won with the largest majority ever received by a New York gubernatorial candidate to that point.

Although women did not have the right to vote, Frank's classmates noted her strong interest in the outcome of the 1882 New

York gubernatorial race. Cleveland frequently sent Frank newspapers, pamphlets, and mementos of events at the governor's mansion.

As both the governor and a longtime family friend, Cleveland had certain built-in advantages toward building a relationship with the young college student. He regularly sent her roses from the governor's greenhouses. In addition to writing her frequently (both Frank and Cleveland were prolific letter writers), Cleveland visited her at Wells during his trips to Buffalo. When her studies permitted, Frank often accompanied the governor on his trips around the state.

One story that Cleveland told following their marriage regarded the time he had visited her at Wells in a driving rainstorm. Frank had just returned to her rooms, and, having been caught in the rain, had struggled to get out of her wet clothing and get dried off. She had no sooner gotten ready to climb into her bed, when she received word that the governor was downstairs. It took her quite a bit of time to get ready, and Cleveland was seen pacing impatiently in the parlor of the residence hall. "A few minutes more," Cleveland would say, "and we might never have been wed."[16]

Most of Frank's classmates considered the weekly flower deliveries and steady correspondence as nothing more than the fatherly attentions of a family friend. Frank herself may have not initially understood Cleveland's motives. But Cleveland knew what he was about.

In 1884, the Democrats nominated Grover Cleveland as their presidential candidate. In those days, candidates did not travel the country, but relied on surrogates to campaign on their behalf. Cleveland might have been able to stay in the background as had his predecessors, were it not for the publication of an item in the Buffalo newspaper with the headline "Terrible Scandal." The article contained the charge by a Buffalo minister that Cleveland had fathered and abandoned an illegitimate child. The birth of Oscar Folsom Cleveland in September 1874, scarcely noted at the time, had now gained national attention.

Cleveland's initial reaction was to deny the tale, but his innate sense of duty ultimately compelled him to instruct his lieutenants to "tell the truth." No less a personage than Henry Ward Beecher took up Cleveland's cause from the pulpit. Beecher's rousing support held a tinge of irony, because Beecher himself had been caught in an adulterous relationship with Elizabeth Tilton in 1871, the result of which had been a scandal that was larger than the one now facing Cleveland.

Emma wrote Frank, expressing her concern for Cleveland's well-being, and added that one had to admire someone who told his advisers to tell the truth. If Emma had already been apprised of the Halpin situation, the revelation would certainly not have come as a shock. If she suspected that her late husband had been the actual father of Halpin's child, she may have been especially grateful for Cleveland's chivalry. Frank, too, had a forgiving attitude toward Cleveland. One of her classmates asked her if the framed photograph of Cleveland hanging on her wall was a picture of her father. No, came the reply, it was a picture of the mayor of Buffalo (namely, Cleveland). "A man more sinned against than sinning," Frank once said, when she read attacks on him in the newspaper.[17]

Frank did not waver in her support of Cleveland. The two continued their active exchange of letters, and she still received a steady stream of flowers, fruits, and political pamphlets from the nation's Democratic presidential nominee.

Frank stayed abreast of the issues during the campaign. The Auburn newspaper, which was delivered to Wells College, had a distinctly Republican outlook. "Early in the campaign," wrote a reporter for the *New York World* several years later, "Miss Folsom became disgusted with its attitude towards Mr. Cleveland and she soon found a subscriber to the *Bulletin*, the Democratic paper, who shared his paper with her. She always waited patiently for its arrival and kept herself pretty well posted on the outlook."[18]

Frank may have had a little touch of "White House fever" as the election season progressed. A letter from another Wells student, dated October 23, 1884, published twenty years later in the *Ladies' Home Journal*, observed:

> I must tell you about one girl here, a Miss Folsom . . . who is awfully nice. She is very handsome, and, my dear, I want you to understand Governor Cleveland is perfectly devoted to her. Sends her flowers all the time, and writes her regularly every week. Of course, she is very much excited to know how the election is coming off, as it will in one case be *slightly* agreeable to her.

I had too much fun with her the other evening. She
said: "Girls, wouldn't it be pretty nice for me to spend a
winter at the White House?" I said, "Why, of course; but
you must be sure to invite all of us to see you."

I am sadly afraid she will never spend such a winter,
aren't you?[19]

Frank and her mother were with Cleveland and his sisters on the
night of the election, but the results were not known that evening. It
took several days for the final tallies to be telegraphed, and Cleveland
wired Frank at Wells when he was confirmed the winner. She and
Kate held a celebration party in their room.

Cleveland invited Emma and Frank to his inauguration, on March
4, 1885, but no president-elect of the United States was going to
overrule Miss Helen Fairchild Smith. The lady dean of Wells refused
Frank permission to attend Cleveland's inaugural, because the dates
conflicted with the school's examination schedule. Frank's first visit
to Washington took place later that month, and it was then that
Cleveland first broached the idea of marriage.

What little has been made public of Frank's diary reveals a typical
young woman with a fresh and inexperienced outlook on the world. "I
can't realize it is Washington. I can't realize it is the White House—or
if it all is, I think I can't be I, but must be some other body."[20]

The available notes from Frank's diary make it unclear as to
whether or not she understood the level of Cleveland's romantic interest
in her. Cleveland had a habit of walking nightly in the White House's
East Room. After dinner, on the first evening of Frank's arrival, she
joined him there. The pair calculated that forty-eight trips from end
to end would make a mile, and they had a view of the moon from
the south window and of an electric light installed outside of the
White House from the north window. Frank wrote: "The president
walks there every night without a light. I suspect I shall not always
have the pleasure of taking it alone with him."[21]

Cleveland, on the other hand, saw himself in the role of
suitor, as Frank discovered that summer when she received his offer
of marriage.

Had Oscar Folsom not died so tragically on that July evening in
1875, Frances Folsom would have likely married Charles Townsend,

or someone else who aspired to the full-time ministry, and Cleveland would have been a close family friend at Frances's wedding. Instead, his role in the lives of the two Folsom women allowed romantic feelings to take root.

Cleveland quietly and assiduously courted Frank, maintaining a protective and quasi-fatherly interest in his former law partner's daughter as she completed her education and matured. Cleveland's courting of Frank was done with her mother's knowledge and both families' evident complicity. If Frank ever considered that she might have had more of a choice, she kept her views to herself. She returned Cleveland's attentions, and just shy of her twenty-second birthday, eleven years after her father's untimely death, she married one of his closest friends.

# 3

# "Her manner is charming"

The newly married Clevelands' special train arrived at the station in a driving rainstorm at four o'clock in the morning. A carriage waited to take them to their bungalow at Deer Park, a resort nestled in Maryland's western mountains owned by Henry G. Davis, a former U.S. senator from West Virginia. The carriage struggled to get through the mud, barely making the short journey without getting stuck. The weather, and the as yet undetected reporters, made an inauspicious beginning for a honeymoon.

Davis offered the location as a honeymoon spot to the president, promising him seclusion, but neither Cleveland nor Davis anticipated the extreme curiosity generated by the president's marriage. Reporters dropped from the trees and assaulted the resort's hotel workers with questions about the newlyweds. Inquisitive journalists lifted the lids of the food being prepared in the hotel kitchen to see what the couple was eating. Reporters badgered workers who came in contact with the Clevelands to find out what they talked about.

Newspapers chronicled every possible detail of the couple's activities. The more respectable newspapers stayed within the bounds of what was considered good taste, but the contrast between the middle-aged, portly president and his young, attractive "ward"-turned-bride was too salacious to ignore completely. One said, "Lights shine dimly at the cottage to-night, suggesting the blaze and crackle of logs in the fireplaces. Whatever may be the condition of the warmth at the cottage, the night outside stimulates a longing for at least two pairs of blankets and a mound of quilts on the bed."[1] Less respectable papers referred to the couple as "beauty and the beast."

Cleveland wrote to Lamont the day after the wedding, expressing his anger toward the intrusiveness of the press into his private life:

> Mr. John Davis came up with us and he has been indefatigable in his efforts to do anything possible for our comfort and pleasure. He brought up with him eight or nine men to act as a patrol charged with the duty of protecting us from newspaper nuisances. He has established certain limits within which such animals are not allowed to enter, and these limits are to be watched and guarded night and day. There are a number of newspaper men here and I can see a group of them sitting on a bridge which marks one of the limits, waiting for some move to be made which will furnish an incident. . . .

Frances also quickly acquired a hostile attitude toward the press, although she became less abrasive in expressing her frustration and anger at reporters' curiosity over the years.

The letter also provides a glimpse of the relationship between the newlywed couple. "You have had so much to do with all that concerned our marriage," Cleveland wrote Lamont, "that we should be glad to have you the first to see us in our new relations. Frank and I have been talking a good deal today about the wedding and in recalling the details of the affair we have run against you so often that I think we are both willing to admit that if it hadn't been for 'poor Colonel Lamont' (as Frank calls you when she recounts all you had to do) we couldn't have been married at all."[2]

By June 5, three days after the nuptials, it was apparent that the newspaper reporters were not going to abandon their posts. Hoping to lessen their intrusiveness, Cleveland invited a select few from the papers he considered to be respectable to talk with him and his bride.

In a well-staged performance, Frank sat at a table, which held a pile of telegrams and letters. Cleveland took a chair near her. He told the reporters that he realized that there was a "pardonable interest throughout the country in regard to happenings here, this interest being wider than he could appreciate."[3] He suggested that writing about the scenery did not provide much in the way of news, and the reporters quickly noted Mrs. Cleveland's laughter at her husband's comment.

Cleveland held out his hand, and Frank placed a batch of telegrams in them. He began to read them silently, selecting those he was willing to share with the assembled group.

The telegrams did not interest the reporters nearly as much as the opportunity to witness the interaction of the president and his new bride. One said, "Her manner toward him was that of a happy but discreet bride, desirous of not appearing too newly wedded, perhaps, but not straining for that effect or losing her composure. The President acted the gentleman at home, attentive and kindly spoken to her as to all, but clearly avoiding any display of his new condition. They would have presented a picture of domestic comfort and happiness not different from this morning's if they had lived together through all the years and in the atmosphere of felicity wished for them by those whose messages they were reading."[4]

That afternoon, the president and his wife dined with the Lamonts, Davises, and other visitors who had accompanied them to church. "The bride picked some wild flowers and whipped the President's chin with them. He stood it as a mastiff regards the playfulness of a cocker spaniel, plainly thinking it very nice for her and harmless to him."[5] It was the type of outward show of affection sought by the omnipresent reporters.

President Cleveland and Colonel Lamont left the women on Monday morning to go on a fishing trip. Reporters determined that the honeymoon was over. Without much fodder for news, the journalists could do little but watch Frank and Mrs. Lamont spend the day sitting on the verandah, followed by a carriage ride and visit later in the afternoon.[6]

The journalists correctly read the signs. The Clevelands and Lamonts left Deer Park the following day, disappointing the hundreds of people who still hoped for a glimpse of the new first lady. Cleveland arranged for his private carriage to pick up the couple at the Washington train station upon arrival, and police cleared a path to keep onlookers away from the carriage's route. Mrs. Grover Cleveland, as she would be known throughout the rest of her life, had achieved instant celebrity status.

The Washington that was to be Frances Cleveland's new home differed vastly from the glamorous and sophisticated European capitals of her recent travels. "Washington is a city of boardinghouses," wrote Frank Carpenter, a correspondent for the *Cleveland Leader* who chronicled the nation's capital as a correspondent, writing under the byline "Carp's Washington." "In respect to the social relation, Washington is one of the wickedest cities of its size in the country. It is natural it should be so for the bulk of the population here are transients. They are away from home; most are far from their families; many have few friends and acquaintances."[7]

Cleveland's election in 1884 ended twenty-four years of Republican rule, bringing with it a true housecleaning of members of Congress, lobbyists, and general hangers-on who benefited from what little government largesse was available at the time. Most Washington denizens thought of time in two-year increments, bounded by the elections, which subjected all members of the House and one-third of the Senate to voter scrutiny.

Permanent residents were often members of the diplomatic corps, and many of them viewed posting to the United States as a stepping-stone to more glamorous careers in Europe's capitals. A permanent bureaucracy remained following the end of the Civil War, created by federal Reconstruction policies, and maintained by the very spoils system that Cleveland had been elected to eradicate.

Provincial though it may have been, Washington society had high expectations of the president's lady, and all eyes were on Frances to see how she would conduct herself. In this regard, the president was no help. He immediately returned to his usual routine, with his days consumed with meetings, dealing with office seekers, and poring over the wording of legislation sent to him by Congress for his signature. Cleveland was a micromanager, and refused to delegate work if he thought the responsibilities were his. Although he had agonized over Frank's life in the White House in his letters to his sisters, Cleveland was typical of most husbands in assuming that his wife could simply figure out how to "handle" the job.

Out of deference to Frank's marriage and new position, Rose had left Washington and returned to her work as a writer and college instructor. Emma returned to Buffalo for the summer.

Flora Payne Whitney stepped in to introduce the young bride to the ways of Washington's elite. Flora enjoyed society, was considered a born diplomat, and had the money to spend on lavish entertainments. Her father was a United States senator. Her brother, Oliver Hazard Payne, had sold his refinery to John D. Rockefeller in the early 1870s, in exchange for which he received a substantial sum, as well as stock and an executive position in the newly consolidated Standard Oil. Oliver had shared his wealth with his sister. Sixty thousand guests allegedly passed through her doors during Whitney's tenure in Cleveland's cabinet.[8]

The British diplomat Cecil Spring-Rice, a friend of the Republican fixtures John Hay, Henry Adams, and Theodore Roosevelt, met the Whitneys shortly after he arrived in Washington in 1887. Writing to a friend, Spring-Rice described the couple: "The Secretary [of the Navy, Whitney] keeps open house, or rather open cottage, and everyone who goes there has anything to eat, drink or smoke that they can wish. He is a clever lawyer who has married an enormously rich (and fat) lady with whose money he is gaining popularity and influence. They are both perfectly kind and the reverse of snobbish. I must say I have seen nothing like that here. The richest people live in the quietest way and only spend money in entertainments and flowers—not in huge houses and gorgeous carriages."[9]

During her first two weeks as the new mistress of the White House, Frances and Flora planned the new first lady's first reception. Two weeks after her wedding anniversary, Frank made her society debut as mistress of the White House. She and the president hosted a formal diplomatic reception, and she was introduced to all the members of the legations represented in Washington. The full cabinet was in attendance, as were hundreds of other invited guests, packed tightly into the Blue Room.

Following the custom of the day, Frances had altered her wedding gown into more useful wear. She wore the dress, with most of the ornaments and bridal trimmings removed, to the reception. A diamond necklace, a gift from her husband, sparkled around her neck. Attendees were especially aware of her wedding and engagement rings, which could be seen through her lace gloves.

Frank demonstrated every ounce of her poise and skill, clearly no longer the inexperienced schoolgirl of the previous year: "The expressions of admiration over Mrs. Cleveland's beauty were on every lip. Society women touched one another and gave an expressive look as they recognized the presence in the White House of one of the prettiest women in America. Her manner is charming, bright and attractive to an unusual degree and her responses to the cordial congratulations were as hearty as could be desired. She was entirely self-possessed and went through the trying ordeal of being stared at by hundreds of the most critical eyes in Washington society without showing a tremor of feeling."[10]

Frances Folsom Cleveland was an overnight social success.

While Flora Whitney attended to Frank's society education, Colonel Lamont tutored her on dealing with a demanding public. As the president's wife, Frank immediately started receiving a daily barrage of letters from well-wishers, admirers, people who wanted permission to paint her portrait, and people who wanted to meet her. One letter, written within a few weeks of her marriage, asked if the writer and her little friends could please meet the president's new wife and shake her hand. Still learning the ropes, Frank scrawled across the top of the letter, "Does this require attention?" At the bottom, Lamont wrote, "Impossible for Mrs. C to find any time other than her receiving hours. Let them come on Mondays or Thursdays [the days in which she held receptions open to the public]."[11]

As the country gradually adjusted to the realities of a married chief executive, it began to look for subtle signs of Frank's influence on their president. Observers quickly noticed that Cleveland now wore a boutonniere whenever his wife carried flowers when they went out for the evening. They attended the theater regularly. For Cleveland, who, in private, was known as an entertaining raconteur and mimic, it had previously been an unheard-of occurrence. For Frank, theater remained a lifelong passion.

The president had a prodigious appetite for long work hours, but he now stopped in the late afternoon to go on a carriage ride with his wife. The practice became so regular between the two that the papers commented when he gave up the rides so that Mrs. Folsom could accompany Frank on the afternoon outings.

The most noticeable change was in Cleveland's attitude. People saw more of his clever sense of humor, and less of his typical gruffness. "He seemed as happy as a man in the back country districts who had suddenly 'got religion,' and got it thoroughly," observed Colonel W. H. Crook, who served in the White House under all of the presidents from Abraham Lincoln to Theodore Roosevelt. [12]

The differences between Frank and her predecessor, Cleveland's sister, Rose, were readily identified within a month of Frank's becoming first lady. Frank held midday receptions in the early afternoon on Tuesdays and Thursdays. Unlike Rose, who would meet with only one person at a time during a reception, Frank was comfortable conversing with her callers, even a few at a time. "A good many pretty well-mannered people did not know how to get out after a polite dismissal [from Rose], and could not be said to carry away entirely agreeable impressions. Mrs. Cleveland, on the contrary, is candid enough to admit she likes to talk to people, is perfectly willing that they enjoy the few minutes they spend with her and receives her callers without a trace of formality or any suggestion that it is the first lady of the land who is giving audiences."[13]

After forty-five years of service in the White House, Crook wrote in his memoirs, "I am an old man now and I have seen many women of various types through all the long years of my service in the White House, but neither there nor elsewhere have I seen any one possessing the same kind of downright *loveliness* which was as much a part of Mrs. Cleveland as was her voice, or her marvelous eyes, or her warm smile of welcome that instantly captivated every one who came in contact with her."[14]

Early on, people speculated that Frank would replace Daniel Lamont as Cleveland's closest confidante. Reporters, expecting they would have greater knowledge of the inner workings of the White House, journalistically drooled at the prospect. The *Washington Post* said, "Of course Mrs. Cleveland will not be any more communicative in her interviews with the reporters than Colonel Lamont was; but she is no woman if she doesn't have a half dozen confidantes of her own sex to whom she will confide in the strictest confidence all the important secrets that the President trusts her with. It will be the confidential lady friends of the President's wife that the shrewd reporters will cultivate."[15]

The press underestimated their quarry. This was the woman who at the youthful age of twenty had managed to conceal her engagement to the president of the United States for nearly a year. Prior to that, she artfully hid the budding romantic relationship with him from all but her closest and most trusted friends. As Crook noted, "While she naturally deferred to her husband's judgment in many matters, Mrs. Cleveland was possessed of a keen mind, and could see straight through things which would baffle many women." She was not fooled by the press's attentions.[16]

In subsequent years, Frank would play a key role in hiding the true condition of her husband's health from a nation in the throes of a potentially crippling financial crisis. Until her own death, Frances Cleveland carefully concealed from the public whatever it was that she did not want them to know about her, or hers.

Frank's new life quickly fell into a pattern of receptions, letter writing, and social visits. The Clevelands' second formal reception, which was open to the public, took place just two days after the diplomatic affair. She again wore her altered wedding dress and her diamond necklace. That evening, the new first lady shook nearly forty-six hundred hands. (By the final end of the Cleveland White House years, Frank's right hand would be a half-size larger than her left, and she would hide her right hand in photographs.)[17]

Frank gave her first formal interview to a newspaper reporter just three and a half weeks after her marriage. She immediately impressed the reporter with her self-confidence and optimistic outlook. "Oh, I just loved the house from the first time I was here. . . . And now they talk of changing the house. I hope they won't. The furnishings might be refreshed, but the house is all I could wish it to be."

Frank continued in a similar, upbeat tone, sharing how much she enjoyed the receptions and the opportunity to meet people, engage in small talk, and watch them. Of course, the public was fascinated by her relationship with the president, but here Frank demonstrated her own skill at deflecting inappropriate curiosity.

"The President is always busy," she said. "I do not see how he accomplishes so much. He sits up to midnight almost every night, but then we do not breakfast until 9 o'clock." In true wifely fashion she then added, "I have him take a nap every day after luncheon or before dinner. . . . I try to have him take as much exercise as I can manage. He walks with me upon this south portico and in the East Room a great deal, but of course that is not outdoor exercise." Then, as if to allay concerns about the president's regimen, Frank carefully adds, "But when we go to the farm he walks all about there, and it rests a man's mind to talk of potatoes and hay and corn and where he is going to put roads and all that."

The interview ended with a discussion of the formal photographs that the new first lady had sat for, and how true to her image they were.[18]

Two months after her wedding date, Frank moved her membership to the First Presbyterian Church, in Washington, DC, where Dr. Byron Sunderland, the man who had performed her wedding ceremony, was the pastor. Cleveland, although the son of one minister and the brother of another, did not retain formal ties to the church. Her mother accompanied Frank to the service.

As usual, reporters were present to chronicle the smallest detail of the first lady's church attendance. When it came time for Communion, members of the congregation waited until the cup from which Frank had been served could be passed to them. The resulting congestion delayed the timely completion of the service.

Cleveland responded with his typical anger at the lack of privacy for his wife in church. His growing bitterness toward the persistent intrusions of the press is reflected in a letter to his Buffalo friend Dr. S. B. Ward, one of the friends who would join him on his upcoming summer vacation.

Cleveland looked forward to getting away from Washington and enjoying his usual pastimes of hunting and fishing. He chose a place in the Adirondacks range in New York, and wrote Ward that a Chicago newspaper had contacted Lamont asking for permission for a reporter to accompany the couple:

My destination will be pretty well known, I suppose, and I begin to fear that the pestilence of newspaper correspondent will find its way to our retreat. And Mrs. Cleveland's presence will, I presume, increase this probability." Cleveland speculates on inviting one reporter who can give to the Associated Press "all that can by any possibility interest any decent citizen of the United States, and giving it out that all other reports are spurious. One thing is certain. If the newspaper men get there, *I shall leave.*

I will not have my vacation spoiled by being continually watched and lied about, and I won't subject my wife to that treatment.[19]

The Clevelands left Washington in mid-August. They embarked by train toward Saratoga, New York, accompanied by Colonel Lamont, Dr. Ward, and three other unidentified friends. Frank's mother joined the group upon their arrival upstate.

In spite of Cleveland's threats, press coverage of the couple's time away was detailed and intrusive.

By the end of the Clevelands' vacation and with their return to Washington, the public had acquired an insatiable appetite for anything they could learn about Frank. Any news about her sold papers, so even the smallest details, such as her monthly shopping trips and personal visits outside of Washington, were chronicled with considerable detail. Consumer products' corporations introduced their wares with labels that boasted the first lady's likeness.

Cleveland's frustration grew in conjunction with the requests for Frances's time, generated by her growing popularity across the nation. Cleveland had not anticipated that the "American Sovereigns" would become enchanted with his wife. But confronted with the reality, Cleveland responded to his wife's immense popularity with characteristic bluntness: "The people of the country insist upon having everything nearly that their President can give—all his time—all his strength and as much as they can get of his home life. I do think he ought to be allowed to have his wife, perhaps not so fully as the humblest citizen, but to some extent."[20]

Cleveland was convinced that his views were the correct ones, and his anger clouded his political judgment. The result was to build a steady stream of public resentment at his intransigence. When friends of the New York City Fire Department invited Frank to visit the city and present a set of flags purchased for the department, she declined the invitation because Cleveland had not been invited, as well: "It would certainly afford me pleasure to contribute in any degree to the significance of this occasion, and to the satisfaction of the brave and gallant men whose services are thus to be recognized. I hope, however, that I shall not be misunderstood when I base my declination of your kind invitation upon my unwillingness to assume that I, as the wife of the President, ought to participate in a public ceremony in which he takes no part."[21]

New York City officials accused the president of being jealous of his wife, because he was not invited to participate in the event. Cleveland strongly denied the accusation, and responded as follows to a letter to George Hepmouth of the New York Fire Department, regarding a letter Cleveland received from Henry Beekman, president of the New York City Board of Aldermen: "The question presented to Mrs. Cleveland was whether she was willing to assume such a public role entirely independent of her husband, and not as an adjunct or incident to something he was to do. Her judgment and feeling were very against it, and she declined the invitation. I am very glad she did, because if the plain meaning of her declination is distorted I am sure her conduct would have been if she had accepted."[22]

Cleveland picked an unlikely venue in which to express his wrath at the newspapers that were practicing "Paul Pry journalism"—a reporting style that delved into the private lives of public people and printed every detail without consideration for the proprieties of the day. The publisher Joseph Pulitzer had introduced the style in the early 1880s, and although Pulitzer had supported Cleveland for president, Cleveland did not appreciate the publisher's journalistic methods.

In October 1886, the president and Mrs. Cleveland were invited to help celebrate the 250th anniversary of the founding of Harvard University. During the evening on which Cleveland addressed the attendees, he glanced at the women's gallery, in which his wife sat. Below him, at the front of the audience, was a row of newspapermen. Departing from his planned remarks, Cleveland said, in a voice shaking with outrage, "O those ghouls of the press," and then continued with denunciatory comments regarding the press coverage that he had received.

Cleveland was quick to recover his composure, and he noted that while he had no problem having his acts as president questioned and criticized by the press, he drew a line at coverage of his personal life. He had "no desire to check the utmost freedom of criticism of all his official acts, but as President he should not be put beyond the protection which fair play should accord every American citizen. . . . [T]he silly, mean, and cowardly lies that every day are found in the columns of certain newspapers . . . violate every instinct of American manliness, and in ghoulish glee desecrate every sacred relation of private life."[23]

For whatever reasons, Cleveland failed to understand that he had a wife who could make his life easier politically, just as she had already proven able to do domestically. Rather than encourage her to use her obvious social skills to build bridges and aid him in developing necessary political alliances, he railed against an intrusive press and an inquisitive public. For a man whose rise to national power had been meteoric, it was an uncharacteristically narrow political strategy. But his idea of womanhood was locked in an antebellum fixation on womanly virtue, a view he was still espousing in 1903, when he wrote for the *Ladies' Home Journal* that a woman's rightful place was as the moral compass of the home. "It is a thousand pities that all the wives found in such company [of "radical" suffragists] cannot sufficiently open their minds to see the complete fitness of the homely definition which describes a good wife as 'a woman who loves her husband and her country with no desire to run either.' " He maintained that women's virtue would be sullied if they were given the right to vote. "Women change politics," he had written, "less than politics change women."[24]

There is every indication that Frances wholeheartedly shared her husband's views on women, and she was surrounded by other women who agreed. Her mother, Helen Fairchild Smith, the Lamonts, the Whitneys, and later the Gilders reinforced the idea that a woman's place was truly in the home. At a time when the role of women in American life was coming under increasing scrutiny, Frances did more than simply avoid the growing public debate. She acted as if there were not even any issues to discuss.

# 4

# "She'll do!"

By the end of 1886, it was clear to the American public that it had a warm, personable, and socially adept first lady. Newspapers wrote glowing descriptions of her gowns, her patronage of the theater, and her softening influence on the president.

Attendance at White House social events skyrocketed, as people took advantage of the opportunity to come in contact with the young Mrs. Cleveland. Frances's Saturday afternoon receptions attracted many of the working women who could not attend her Tuesday and Thursday events. As many as nine thousand people attended one reception, and many of those nine thousand returned to the end of the line and waited for a chance to greet Frances again.

Even Frances's mother, who hovered worriedly over her daughter as she went about her duties, relaxed her vigilance. Just a few short months following the Clevelands' marriage, Emma interrupted a meeting of the president's to urge him to check on Frances's deportment during a reception. Angry at the intrusion, Cleveland gruffly responded, "She'll do!" And, when she double-checked on her daughter, Emma saw that he was right.

Americans who could not travel to Washington reached out to Frances with letters. Her mail became filled with requests from economically struggling and impoverished women throughout the nation asking her to send money, help them with their marriages, or find jobs. The most frequent request was for Frances to intervene with the president to secure their husbands' employment as postmasters. (Civil

service reform was in its earliest stages of discussion at this time, and
the position of local postmaster was still a patronage job, obtained by
appointment of the president of the United States.)

A typical letter read:

> Knowing you have a good Christian heart and character
> I feel you will not cannot resist this appeal, were I but
> present *I would ask this on my knees*. I come before you,
> the wife of Colonel W. B. Hayward, *pleading* with you to
> ask your dear husband (Honorable President of our beloved
> United States) if he will give my husband a position of
> some kind that will enable him to support me, his wife,
> and our three children.
>
> . . . Pardon me for thus addressing you, but could you,
> a *true, noble-hearted woman*, but know our great distresses,
> anxieties and actual suffering, even for daily bread.[1]

Sometimes, women wrote on their own behalf, asking Frances
to intervene to secure them employment.

> Mrs. President Cleveland:
>
> I earnestly solicit your influence in my behalf in
> having the Post Office established which is considered an
> urgent necessity. Enclosed papers will inform you. Hoping
> your influence with our President, and Postmaster Villas,
> will be a success. If I am appointed I will do everything
> in my power to give you entire credit. The position will
> suit me, and my husband will take charge if considered
> more suitable, his health is delicate.
>
> I am determined to persevere on account of my
> children. God will reward your influence. My children
> and myself will look forward to the appointment. I wish
> I could take hold of your hand and ask you in person.
> I will not mention if I am successful, for fear others will
> trouble you, but by permission. It will be a special favor
> to the Teachers of the Public Schools of Philadelphia with
> whom I served for fifteen years.[2]

These letters were routinely answered by one of the president's secretaries, although not without the occasional comment or suggestion from Frances, who read through all of her mail. A Georgia woman wrote that she had a "girlish fancy" and would like to be married in a dress that Mrs. Cleveland had used. A terse note, written across the top of the letter, says, "Mrs. Cleveland has no dresses not in use. FC."[3]

When Frances received a letter addressed to "Fannie Cleveland," in which the writer asked for help in locating some lost Folsom relatives who had moved to California, Frances directed a secretary as follows, "Refer her to book called The Folsom Genealogy compiled by Jacob Chapman of Exeter, N.H. which will give her more information than I can. FC."[4]

Frances's public life meant that she was never alone, but there were signs that she was lonely. The afternoon carriage rides and trips to the theater with Cleveland (although one White House guest noted that the president looked as if he were being taken to the gallows) gave her some personal time with her husband.[5] But she spent many evenings alone, looking for other companionship.

In March, before he and Frank married, Cleveland had purchased a home where the two of them could retreat from the demands of White House life. It was an unusual decision, as no president had maintained another residence in Washington since the White House had been reoccupied following its burning during the War of 1812. Cleveland found a small home on the Tenallytown Road, situated near Georgetown, about three miles from the White House.

The property, called "Oak View" by the Clevelands, and christened "Red Top" by the press because of its red-painted roof, was located near the Whitneys' home.[6]

This was how Sir Cecil Spring-Rice first made her acquaintance: ". . . I am still staying at the 'Whitney Farm' as it is called here. The air is several degrees cooler and life very cheerful. There is a sort of cabinet meeting there, as the Secretary of War, of the Navy, and of the Treasury are staying. Mrs. Cleveland came last night; as the President, whose country place is next, was working too hard to speak to her . . . she 'thought she'd drop in.' She is a tall, very pretty and direct person."[7]

Spring-Rice also discovered Frances's sense of humor, as well as her well-concealed interest in politics.

> She had just been [on] a tour in the North with the President. She said she had to get accustomed to people saying they were discontented with her looks—which she said was natural, as one eyelid was bitten and was as big as an egg and she had to have it bandaged. "Which was a great pity," she said, "as, of course, the President was there for his talking and I for my looks. And the President had a sore throat."
>
> She said she had a great trouble on her mind. The President had gone on the loose and bought himself an orange tawny linen suit. He now threatened to wear it. She had used every artifice in her power to prevent it. "What would he look like in it, think?" . . . At last he found it so hot that he had said he *must* wear it. So, she told him he would certainly lose the Irish vote if he wore a yellow suit, and this argument prevailed.[8]

In 1887, Wells College named Helen Fairchild Smith and Frances as the first women trustees of the school. Frances traveled to Wells in mid-June to attend the school's commencement and attend a trustees' meeting. The commencement speaker was Richard Watson Gilder, a poet and editor of *Century* and *Scribners* magazines. He and Frances struck up an immediate friendship, and Gilder accompanied her back to Washington at the end of the week's events to meet the president.

Gilder and Cleveland were similar in several ways. Natives of New Jersey, both men had overcome impoverished upbringings to achieve prominence in their respective fields. As was typical of most of those in his social and professional circles, Gilder was a Republican because it was the antislavery party of Lincoln. But, typical of many of the Republicans in 1884 who were tired of Republican-led corruption in Washington, Gilder had supported Cleveland, and had used his publications' influence during the 1884 election to garner support for the Democratic candidate.

Gilder's circle included the nation's aristocratic intelligentsia. He was a close friend of Henry Adams, the grandson of John Quincy Adams and great-grandson of John Adams. Gilder published Adams' writings, including selections from his monumental history of the United States that covered the times of Jefferson and Madison.

Mark Twain was another close friend of Gilder, who published Twain's work, and Gilder introduced the author to the presidential couple. While Twain and the Clevelands never developed the close relationship that the latter had with the Gilders, he did maintain contact with them from time to time.

Gilder's wife, Helena deKay Gilder, was a noted painter and founder of the Society of American Artists and the Art Students League. Both institutions broke the power held over American artists by the National Academy of Design, which represented the nation's artistic old guard. Prior to her marriage, deKay had studied with Winslow Homer and John LaFarge. LaFarge was an artist who was perfecting the techniques of stained glass in artwork, and he created a stained glass window for Wells College, which still exists on the campus. LaFarge used a photo of Frances from her Wells days as the model for the Aurora window. Another member of deKay's circle was Augustus Saint-Gaudens, who was gaining recognition as an outstanding sculptor; he eventually became friends with Frances.

The Gilders' New York home was a salon for many of the nation's literary and visual artists. Their summer home in Buzzards Bay, Massachusetts (known back then as "Buzzard's Bay"), included Helena's studio, where she worked and entertained. It would not be long before Frances would become a frequent guest.

Gilder was smitten with the young Mrs. Cleveland. Within a day of leaving Washington, he wrote:

June 29, 1887.
My dear Mrs. Cleveland,
        . . . . I find that Mr. Scott (treasurer and trustee of the Century Company) met you somewhere in Italy—without knowing anything of you but your name— . . . He was travelling with Mrs. Scott, for her health. . . . and many they are—who like you without the aid of a national glamour.

Gilder mentions the idea of a proper portrait being painted of Frances. He suggests the "American-European Sargent" ("whose work you probably know") as one possibility, and then mentions St. Gaudens. "St. Gaudens is . . . one of the best [sculptors] now living. Beside his public work—The Farragut in New York—the forthcoming Col. Shaw in Boston and Lincoln in Chicago, etc., he has made some most exquisite portraits in the style I speak of."[9]

Gilder suggests that, as an alternative, Frances or her friends or the president consider having St. Gaudens do her portrait, which would require "sittings during two weeks in Washington or wherever you prefer."[10]

Gilder's interest in immortalizing Mrs. Cleveland in paint or bronze contrasts with the contents of a letter Frank sent him on the same day. In it, she asks him to assist her in having an advertisement for face powder that uses her image removed from the *Century Magazine.*

"Would you mind, my dear Laureate," she wrote, "if I ask a favor and I know you will be good to grant it. I find the enclosed advertisement in the June Century. My attention was called to it today. I don't like it any more than you [will] when you learn of it. These people sent me a box of their perfumes long ago for which I thanked them—and now they are advertising their face powder as being used by me also. Can you have it taken out?"[11]

Frances's newfound relationship with Gilder offered her a small opportunity to try to stop the inappropriate use of her image in advertising. Her nearly overnight celebrity status occurred at the same time that the American consumer goods industry was just beginning to grow. Manufacturers had learned that advertising, complete with exaggerated claims about the efficacy of their products, boosted sales. Companies that made everything from liver and arsenic pills to tobacco products, luggage, sewing machines, and soaps freely appropriated Frances's name and image to hawk their wares.

Cleveland supporters in Congress expressed outrage at the use of Frances's image. Such conduct was considered unchivalrous toward a lady, and a bill was introduced forbidding the unapproved use of any image of any American woman. The legislation was not enacted, in part because Cleveland's relationship with Congress was so poor that its members were unwilling to give him even a small legislative victory.

Cleveland frequently lost his temper when he learned of inappropriate uses of his wife's image in a "most indecent way." He wrote the publisher of the *Albany Evening Journal* in regard to one such advertisement: "I suppose we must always have . . . dirty and disreputable fellows, but I shall be surprised if you find such advertising profitable. . . ."[12]

Cleveland's attempts to defend the honor of his wife were no recompense for the increasing loneliness she experienced in the White House. In the same letter to Gilder, Frances mentions her boredom, a theme that emerges among her confidantes. Rainy weather has confined her indoors in the White House, and the only pastime was to play with her dogs.

> I think I have to go into photography just to be able to catch my three dogs when I have a good chance. Kay [one of her dogs] was horribly jealous and whined and cried like a baby. I must tell you Kay cries when I kiss the President and the other day he almost ate up a small baby of first months which I took in my arms [at a reception].
> This is a protest letter and dog letter.[13]

The relationship between Gilder and Frances developed quickly. The following day, he wrote in response to an even earlier letter that he had received from her. Judging by Gilder's tone, it appears that someone wrote to Frances and suggested that her behavior with Gilder at Wells was not entirely proper. Gilder moved quickly to squelch any hint of impropriety.

> Your instincts are as usual correct. I am (not) sorry to say that this lady is unknown to me, and it goes without saying that her action is totally without authority from me. It is evidently a trick. With such material as this secured from you she would have a first rate card, and means of access to the periodicals.
> One of the incidents you mention is, I suppose, the necessity of a certain complaisance in directions where you would choose to act otherwise—but this writer who professes so much loyalty to you and wishes thereby to impose upon your good nature evidently does not understand that

the public—i.e. the self-respecting public—would always support you in your usual and natural reticence as to details of your private life.

Mrs. Gilder and I held a . . . meeting on reading the letter you enclosed from this extraordinary person. I am deeply grateful to you for communicating at once with me; my first thought was to telegraph to yourself or to Col. Lamont—being determined that the faint possibility of such an impertinence should not rest for an hour longer—upon myself or the Century. But I feared that the telegraph might "leak" somewhere and your name be "taken in vain."[14]

By the end of the summer of 1887, Frances had established a strong correspondence and was nurturing a growing friendship with both Gilders. Letters exchanged during this time period give the impression of a sense of relief on Frances's part that she had found friends who enjoyed her for her intellect and her personality, who would keep confidences and offer her outlets for her many literary and artistic interests.

In the early fall, the Clevelands embarked on a tour of western and southern states. Neither region enjoyed the post-Reconstruction economic resurgence that was creating wealth in the northeastern and mid-Atlantic states. Western farmers faced exorbitant rail fees to ship their produce to the more populous East, and southerners struggled with the economic challenges of farming large acreage without the use of enslaved labor.

For the Clevelands, the trip was a goodwill tour, and the one member of the traveling party who generated the most goodwill was Frances. Large crowds turned out along carriage routes, at rallies, and along the rail lines, all with the hope of catching a glimpse of the enormously popular president's wife.

Frances took the outpouring of support in stride. In a response to Gilder's concerns for her safety after a large crowd surged toward the Cleveland party's carriages in Madison, Wisconsin, she wrote: "Pray don't be concerned about a body guard for us in our travels. We are splendidly looked after—the papers [exaggerate] even with the overwhelming amount of harrowing details at their disposal. I wasn't ill at all in Chicago—and the crowds were very nicely managed. . . . We had more fun getting back to Palmer House than all the state of a procession could have afforded us. It was one of the experiences of the trip and nowadays when Col. Lamont, Dr. Bryant and I hide out in a carriage in a crowd we have a policeman on the box."[15]

A week later, the entourage stopped in Tennessee on its way to visit Atlanta. Frances wrote to Helena: "Just a note to tell you I am still enjoying myself very much and still thinking very often and very lovingly of you and My Laureate. We have spent Tuesday—delightfully—and are quite rested to attack Atlanta tomorrow night. Atlanta means very home in a *relative time*. I am a trifle wearied with so much glory . . . I suffer too much fearing some little child will get run over in the immense crowds and yet it will be a glorious memory in total."[16]

Upon her return to Washington, Frank penned a note to "Dear Helena—and Dear 'My Laureate' ":

> It has all been wonderful—an experience worth much more than we have seen in undertaking it. And isn't the greatest wonder of all the fact that so few accidents have occurred in connection with it—where so many thousands of people have been crowded together so many houses have been frantic—and there has been so much —— (?) at confusion. I can't see how someone was not killed. Do you know the constant strain on my nerves lest some one should be trampled upon nearly wore me out at first? But I saw that no body did get stepped on—and no body's limbs were crushed—to say nothing of their *skulls*. . . .[17]

That Thanksgiving, Frances's close friends from Wells—Julia Severance, Virginia Kingsford, and Minnie Alexander—spent the 1887 Thanksgiving holiday with the Clevelands at the White House. Julia, who was a prolific diarist, chronicled her stay and offers some interesting glimpses of the Clevelands' life.

> A glass of milk in Frank's little parlor stayed us until Mary, the housekeeper, and our deft-handed Phyllis pro tem, helped us to dress for dinner. Then came the ordeal—how

to meet the President, how to address him and how to conduct ourselves. But the hearty greeting settled all doubts at once, and Virginia upon one arm and myself upon the other, he led the way downstairs to dinner. . . . Then Beverly, Isaiah and William ministered to our real and imaginary wants, and the President proceeded to prove that he was not such a formidable object, after all.

With his hand to guide, not the ship of State, but the Elevator, we all ascended to Frank's little parlor where we grouped ourselves about the President who reclined in our midst. But he measured his cosy time by the length of the segar, and that finished, bade us goodnight, and went to his office.

The next day, Sunday, Frank and her friends attended church, minus the president. [T]he President professed to have such a headache that he could not possibly sit through a service, so though we had hoped to appear under his escort, we girls were compelled to go without him.

. . . Frank sat in the corner of the President's pew listening intently.[18]

The young women traveled to the Clevelands' country home, Oak View, with Frank driving herself and Julia "in the buggy with the beautiful new horse Lady Palmer." Julia wrote, "Frank proved a gallant horsewoman, and though Lady Palmer showed great spirit, we dashed by the others and drove up to the Farm some minutes in advance."[19]

Cleveland was there to join them for lunch, his headache apparently gone.

Like Frank several years earlier, Julia was treated to a walk in the White House's East Room with Cleveland after dinner that evening. "Indeed," writes Julia, "I must not forget to mention my pleasant walk in the East Room with the President. We sauntered in after dinner, and after our little chat in the dark, pacing to and fro, in spite of the fact that the others wished themselves in my shoes, and came out the best of friends. At least such was my feeling, and I hope it was not far from correct."[20]

Cleveland continued to make an effort to be sociable with Frank's closest circle of friends. On Monday evening, he accompanied the group to the theater, although, as Julia writes,

> [T]he poor President, with a look of grim endurance, escorted us all to the Opera House to see Mansfield as Dr. Jekyll and Mr. Hyde. Colonel and Mrs. Lamont, with the Rogers, Mrs. Folsom and "we girls" did well toward filling the two boxes at north of the stage. . . .
> . . . [B]ut there was plenty of staring at Mr. and Mrs. President. Mr. Mansfield had left an enormous bouquet of roses on the railing in front of Frank, who gave them loving touches and a cordial acceptance."

After the performance, the actor visited with Frank, while the other three young women visited with an acquaintance.[21]

For Frank, Thanksgiving Day was a respite from her official activities. "We had a pleasant homelike Thanksgiving at Oak View," she wrote the Gilders, "and we have been having a quite delightful little visit all by ourselves that is without any society nonsense."[22]

The last entry of Julia's diary, dated December 5, 1887, notes that Cleveland read the women the speech he was to deliver to Congress in the morning.

With the departure of her friends, Frank once again faced the loneliness and boredom that were becoming a staple of her White House life. As Christmas approached, she wrote Helena:

> I suppose I am a terrible nuisance to both of you, I send you lines so often. Today—or until today I've been very patient—But now I want to see *if* I can't say something to make you say something to me. The Marcus Aurelius came yesterday—I shall learn to be very fond of it before Christmas. And then I shall many and many a time read a thought at a time to my dear husband. He will be pleased I foresaw—I have been reading some of Miss Lazarus's poems from the books you brought me Helena dear—and have just finished the Dance to Death. How powerful it

is—I am getting so much enjoyment from the books, for I had known before only here and there a stray poem. Could you send, without too much trouble, the Hebrew American (isn't it?) which contained the different articles about Emma Lazarus—I think I cannot get it here.[23]

The letter ends on a plaintive note: "Please won't you come and see me and tell me something. I want to be talked to—I want to be scolded—I want to be made to do something. Never tell me again any thing I am—but just what I must be. If you two don't make something out of me it is your own faults. I am willing and in your hands—I am drifting right on terribly. . . ."[24]

# 5

# "The place is full of rumours about Mrs. Cleveland"

When Cleveland faced reelection in 1888, he did so with one of the nation's most popular first ladies at his side. The *New York Times* captured America's attitude about Frances: "Other Presidents have shared the honors of the Executive Mansion with wives whose personal attractiveness, accomplishments, wit and tact have commanded admiration, but in not one of all the wives of Presidents have the whole people manifested more interest than they do in the present lady of the White House. . . . Her youth, beauty, grace, animation, and unaffected cordiality were irresistible. These attractions have stood well the test of time. Their possession has won steadily upon the affection of the country."[1]

Frances's popularity was considered a political plus for Cleveland. "She has done much to save the President, standing by his side at four great receptions, and making thousands of people happy with her beautiful smile and cordial shake of the hand."[2]

Cleveland supporters sought to use Frances's widespread public approval to their advantage in the upcoming presidential campaign. Although women could not vote, they organized Frances Folsom Cleveland Clubs "for the purpose of taking an active part in the coming presidential election. . . . The Clubs [are] designed to rally Democratic women around the President's exceedingly popular wife, and encourage support for his re-election."[3]

However, Cleveland, with typical stubbornness and insistence that politics was outside of a woman's sphere of influence, did everything he could to discourage the formation of these clubs. In later years, Cleveland would write: "I am persuaded that without exaggeration of statement we may assume that there are woman's clubs whose objects and intents are not only harmful, but harmful in a way that directly menaces the integrity of our homes and the benign disposition and character of our wifehood and motherhood; that there are others harmless in intent, but whose tendency is toward waste of time and perversion of effort, as well as toward the formation of the club habit. . . ."[4]

Frances shared her husband's views regarding the appearance of women as apolitical, and she did nothing to acknowledge or support the clubs. She shared with Cleveland the view that her sphere of influence was in the home, a sacred place of which she was the keeper and protector.

Frances referred letters to her regarding the clubs to Cleveland, who responded with a surprising degree of tact:

> Mrs. Cleveland has referred me to your letter informing her of the organization of a "Frances Cleveland Influence Club." It is by no means pleasant to dissent from the methods which sincere friends adopt when their efforts not only demonstrate their friendliness, but when they also seek to subserve the public good and are, therefore, engaged in a patriotic service. It is, however, impossible for us to approve the use of Mrs. Cleveland's name in the designation of clubs assigned to do political work. We trust you will not undervalue our objection, because it rests upon the sentiment that the name now sacred in the home circle as wife and mother may well be spared in the organization and operation of clubs created to exert political influence.[5]

Frances's political activities may not have been overt in the manner suggested by a club that bore her name, but she was, in fact, politically astute and active behind the scenes.

One area in which she moved to the forefront of public support was in the efforts under way for the United States to adopt the laws related to international copyright. Without the copyright provisions, American authors lost income whenever their works were published overseas because they were not entitled to receive royalties. In an irony typical of American politics, Congress insisted on retaining tariffs to protect its local industries, but took over ten years of debate before it finally adopted international copyright conventions in 1891, which were, in effect, tariff protection for the nation's authors.

Cleveland supported the passage of copyright legislation, and Frank's strong interest in the arts made her a natural advocate of any law that would promote artistic endeavors. In 1888, supporters gathered to encourage congressional approval of international copyright law. "The Congregational Church on G-street was well filled by an audience of intelligent sympathizers with those American authors who are endeavoring to stimulate popular interest and the attention of Congress in their efforts to secure legislation for enforcing international copyright," the *New York Times* reported. Two of the authors who spoke were close to Frank: Gilder and Samuel L. Clemens. In the audience, as supporters, were Frank, her friend Katherine Willard, who was visiting at the White House, and Mrs. Daniel Lamont.[6] The Clevelands hosted a White House reception for the authors as another show of support for the legislation's passage.

Tariff reform was the primary goal of Cleveland's administration, and Frank appeared with friends in the Senate gallery to hear debate on the subject. Her appearance had little influence on the vote. Cleveland's efforts to reduce tariffs and stimulate economic growth were again defeated by a nonsupportive Congress.

Richard Gilder was one of the few intimates with whom Frances could openly share her political observations. Frank described her assessment of Republican politics as the year 1887 drew to a close and Cleveland worked on his State of the Union message to Congress. "It is not *good* news that you brought me from your Republican Senator—I think our Republican friends are going to try to cajole us into inaction by soft words—and to gain a victory over the Democrats. I trust our people *won't walk* into the trap too easily. Our good President is working away on the message. This is always a sorry time of year in our household."[7]

The Democrats recognized Frances as a political asset at their convention in June 1888. Mrs. Cleveland was said to have "preeminent qualifications as a Democrat," and to have made "strong political friends for her husband, such as he could not possibly have obtained in any other way than through her influence."[8]

The Republicans also recognized Frances's "pre-eminent qualifications," and they sought a tool to discredit Cleveland and tarnish his name with the public. The prominent Republican Chauncey Depew is credited with saying that the Republican nominee would have a hard time running against both Mr. and Mrs. Cleveland.

Given Frances's unprecedented popularity, the easiest and most insidious effort by Cleveland's opponents to smear his reputation was to insinuate that he was brutish and abusive toward his young, charming, and attractive wife.

> The place is full of rumours about Mrs. Cleveland [Sir Cecil Spring-Rice wrote to a friend in a letter dated April 15, 1888]. As she is such a good card for the Democrats to play, the Republicans want to turn it against them and accuse the President of beating his wife. She is said to have fled from Washington in the summer because he became unsupportable and also to have been obliged by him to send away a maid who interfered in her behalf and got a cut on the head with a broomstick.
>
> The fact is that, as anyone can see, they are a most devoted couple and nobody could be more so. But this is a form of politics which, in the absence of more important questions, becomes dominant here.[9]

Depew fueled the gossip by publishing a detailed story of Cleveland's alleged behavior in the *New York World*. Depew reported that Kentucky congressman Watterson, a key ally of Cleveland's in the battle with Congress over tariff reform, escorted Mrs. Cleveland to the theater, and that upon her return to the White House, the president "upbraided her, called her wicked names and finally slapped her face."[10]

Watterson escorted Frances to the theater, and in his account noted that "the President himself did not go because he was so busy with his work." When the theatergoers returned to the White House, Watterson and the president "chatted." The president "laughed good-naturedly and courteously thanked Mr. Watterson for his kindness."[11]

Watterson's story rings true. Frances was a devotee of the theater and once remarked that she would spend every evening there, if she could. Cleveland, who took more time away from his desk in the evenings than he had prior to his marriage, was still duty-driven by the demands of the presidency and often did not escort Frank. The laughter and courtesy described by Watterson were typical of the sociable side of Cleveland's personality.

Watterson's account did not appear until December of that year, leaving the atmosphere ripe for the scandal to escalate. The charges drew a fresh round of attention in late May, when Reverend C. H. Pendleton, a Baptist minister, fanned the rumor flames when his Decoration Day sermon was published in the *Worcester (MA) Telegram.* Newspapers nationwide reprinted the allegations.

In his pulpit message, Pendleton asserted that "Mrs. Cleveland had been forcibly abused by her husband, that her mother, Mrs. Folsom, had been driven from the White House and had gone off to Europe in order to prevent a further scandal."[12]

Pendleton's allegations spurred Richard and Helena Gilder into action. They submitted a letter on June 9 to the *Boston Globe* "from a gentleman and his wife, not in politics, who have seen a great deal of the private life of the White House since the President's marriage":

> My wife and myself heard these libels at first with amusement, then with astonishment and indignation [wrote Gilder]. They are, of course, grotesquely, outrageously, totally false in every respect, both as to the President's habits and as to the relations between himself and his wife. So contented, happy and beautiful a home life as that of the White House it has seldom been our good fortune to witness. The truth about all this is too well known for these libels to live. Under the form of a slander upon the President they are in reality an infamous attack upon the peace and happiness of a woman universally respected and beloved. Our people are too chivalrous to permit this for a moment.[13]

The Gilders were one of the only close friends of the Clevelands to address publicly at the time the falseness of Pendleton's and Depew's charges. Those who knew the most about the Clevelands' private relationship may have felt that a failure to address the allegations, which they knew to be untrue, would cause the furor to die quickly.

In an unprecedented step, Frances responded to a letter written by a Massachusetts woman, Mrs. Maggie Nicodemus, who had heard the charges from Pendleton's pulpit. In her letter, Mrs. Nicodemus asked if Pendleton's statement was true. Frances replied:

> Dear Madam:
>     I can only say in answer to your letter that every statement made by the Rev. C. H. Pendleton in the interview which you sent me is basely false, and I pity the man of his calling who has been made the tool to give circulation to such wicked and heartless lies.
>     I can wish the women of our country no greater blessing than that their homes and lives may be as happy and their husbands may be as kind, attentive, considerate, and affectionate as mine.[14]

A copy of the letter exists in the Grover Cleveland Papers, and it is written in Daniel Lamont's handwriting, not Frances Cleveland's. Researchers cataloging the papers apparently noted this, because a handwritten message at the top reads: "Is this Mrs. Cleveland's writing?" To which another cataloger responded, "No, Lamont's, I think."[15]

Lamont likely composed the letter to go out over Frances's signature. In matters of correspondence where a politically sensitive response, or a negative response, was required, Lamont typically crafted the language. In nearly every one of these instances, Lamont wrote and signed the letter himself. This particular situation is unique, in that Frances most likely recopied Lamont's text into her own handwriting and signed the note to Mrs. Nicodemus. The papers credit Mrs. Nicodemus with releasing Frances's response to them.[16]

Unlike with the stories that circulated during the 1884 election about Cleveland's illegitimate child, newspapers quickly jumped to Frances's defense. The *Times* investigated Pendleton's background and printed an article entitled, "Slandered Jefferson, Too." It reported that Pendleton had preached at a church in Cleveland, and had gone without much notice until he was invited to deliver a speech to the

Lincoln Club in March 1887. In that address, Pendleton reportedly launched a "vicious assault on the memory of Thomas Jefferson, whom he pronounced the most overestimated man of his age, 'the spiritual father of that party whose history is a crime.' " Pendleton described Jefferson as a "crafty, vindictive schemer, and an exceedingly bad man." Pendleton's scurrilous remarks prompted a quick denial from members of the Lincoln Club, and precipitated Pendleton's resignation from his church in Cleveland. Pendleton was characterized as a man whose "tongue was longer than his judgment."[17]

During the time that the story of Cleveland's alleged abuse circulated, Frances continued her typical routine of visits to friends along the Eastern seaboard. Enemies used her trips as further evidence of the truthfulness of their charges. Newspapers friendly to the Clevelands saw no remarkable change in either Frances's appearance or conduct.

With friends in Germantown, Pennsylvania, located near Philadelphia, Frances enjoyed the company of close friends with whom she could easily relax. "It was an agreeable party," the *New York Times* reported of her trip, "made up for the most part of friends whom Mrs. Cleveland had known in her school days. The day and the turnout and the scenery were all that could be desired, everybody was at ease and laughing and chatting without ceremony or restraint, and the change from the formal gathering and surroundings in which the President's wife had been participating seemed to have its full effect upon her."[18]

From Germantown, she traveled to Princeton College, in New Jersey, where a large reception was held in her honor. The gala event included the entire community: professors and their wives, students, and friends of the college's president. "Mrs. Cleveland had a smile for each. When asked if it would tire her to meet all the students she said she would not be satisfied if she did not meet them all. About 800 persons shook hands with her."[19]

Frances's smile still radiates from a photograph taken that day. She is seated at the front of a large group of people, holding an enormous bouquet and wearing a hat adorned with large white flowers. She commented on her smile in a letter to Allan Marquand, the photographer and host of the event. What she called "open-mouthedness" is what we would today call smiling.

Mr. Gilder says as you put the cap on the camera after the first exposure I said, "Oh, my mouth was open"—I think it was!—but I am just as much obliged to you for the photograph—for I was the only open mouthed sitter, and everyone else is pretty good except the aforesaid Mr. Gilder. Your mother's expression of mirth at my open mouthedness is truly laughable, and Mrs. Gilder is as serious as I am silly. It's a pleasant memento of a delightful day and I am greatly obliged—while I sympathize with your accident which befell the other plates. [Marquand broke all the other glass plates of the photos he took of the occasion.]

> Very sincerely,
> Frances F. Cleveland[20]

By the middle of the summer of 1888, news of scandal had quieted to the point that news reporters had very little of importance to write about. Frank was spending her summer with the Gilders at their home in Marion, which she had also done the year before. The papers reported that "[a] relative of Mrs. Cleveland has been looking around Marion and vicinity seeking a purchasable site for a Summer cottage, but so far without success. It is supposed she has been doing so in behalf of the President or his wife. The few people who saw Mrs. Cleveland this morning, and who also saw her one year ago, say that she is looking thinner than when last in the State, and shows signs of needing rest and recuperation."[21]

The merest breath of scandal could no longer be found in Washington during the languid summer days of 1888, necessitating the creation of something newsworthy that involved Frances Cleveland.

According to a story eventually published by the Atlanta *Constitution*, one of its reporters, Colonel Jay Durham, was sitting in the newspaper's Washington office on a rainy Sunday afternoon. "I have a syndicate letter to write," remarked one of the newspaper's correspondents. "Cannot some one suggest a subject?"

"That's the easiest part of the letter," responded Durham. "The labor is in writing it. Take it on a typewriter and I will give you a White House story that will go. Anything about Mrs. Cleveland is good, and I have decided that it would be a good idea to have her discard the bustle. That will set the style, the bustle will go and we democrats will have the satisfaction of driving the protected manufacturers of wire bustles to the wall. Protection must go. If we cannot kill the entire business we will put the knife into a few anyway."

All of the nation's newspapers picked up the story, and even the nation's fashion newspapers decided that abolishing the bustle was a good thing. American women quickly went out to order new dresses designed without the bustle, but Frances, in her typically conservative fashion, continued to shop for clothing with the bustle. This eventually ended when she asked for a bustle in one of Washington's stores.

"A bustle?" exclaimed the young lady clerk in amazement. "Excuse me, Mrs. Cleveland, but we have sent them to the cellar. Since the papers said you had discarded the bustle we have not sold one and have sent them to the cellar to make room for saleable goods. Is it true you have not done so?"

"Don't trouble about going for them," replied Mrs. Cleveland. Then turning to Flora Whitney, she said, "I suppose I shall have to adopt the style to suit the newspapers," and the next day she went to Grimes for new dresses and alterations in the ones she had, but that was a month after the adoption of the style."[22]

The nation thanked her for her "contribution" to fashions. "Mrs. Cleveland has done one good thing for the women of this country. With a wave of the hand she has wiped the bustles off the fashion plates. Indeed, it is really a blessing. Then it is so odd that the president's wife should take the matter in hand. But she has done so. Bustles are only good for masks to be used by the small boys at baseball matches now."[23]

When the election results rolled in, Cleveland had won ninety thousand more votes than his opponent, Benjamin Harrison, grandson of President William Henry Harrison, of "Tippicanoe and Tyler, Too!" fame. But Cleveland had failed to carry his adopted state of New York, and the state's thirty-six electoral votes were tallied in Harrison's column, swinging the election to him.[24]

Frances was described as " 'true grit' all the way through" as she awaited the election returns with friends and family in the White House during the evening after polls had closed. "Mrs. Cleveland and her mother were brave and smiling to the last, and neither showed by the least word their great disappointment."[25]

Frank publicly handled the disappointment in her typical, matter-of-fact fashion: "I am sorry for the president; and for his sake wish it had been otherwise, but what cannot be helped must be met."

Friends expressed their wish that Frances would stay in Washington after the end of their White House tenure in March. "Too early to talk of that," smilingly replied Mrs. Cleveland. "We love our country home here and we love New York, and we women follow our husband's fortunes, you know."[26]

A week later, Frank had resumed her typical activities, this time working on behalf of her alma mater, Wells College. As president of the Eastern Association of Wells College, Frances conducted a meeting to outline activities to raise funds to replace the campus buildings that had been destroyed by fire. Members agreed to solicit funds individually, receiving subscriptions from donors. "Mrs. Cleveland consented to receive such subscriptions, and although the task of acknowledging remittances will no doubt prove an onerous one, she cheerfully agreed to do so over her own signature, however small the amounts."[27]

With the election over and the knowledge that Frances would no longer be in the White House, newspapers scrambled to write as many stories about her as they could. One reporter had an interview with her mother, Emma Folsom, who spoke with embarrassing candor about her daughter:

> You will never hear anything imprudent emanating from Mrs. Cleveland. She is wonderfully prudent and cautious in all her words and conduct. The president has the greatest of blessings in his young wife, and he is in his heart too happy to be long cast down by political fortune. Though older, considerably, than she, he does not permit her to realize it, and her affection for him is extreme. Do you remember George Eliot's saying that the happiest wife is she who finds combined in her husband the tenderness of a father with the devotion of a husband? Mrs. Cleveland looks up to her husband with the trust and confidence she felt as a child in him, and she is very proud of her heart's choice.[28]

Emma was asked about the rumors regarding the president's cruel conduct of her daughter, and she denied their veracity. "He is not so ambitious in any direction as he is for the happiness of the beautiful girl who made a hero of him before she was out of short dresses; and who looks at him through the glamour of love's young dream. The only comfort I find in the defeat of the president is that the public will have the opportunity to correct some misapprehensions entertained toward him and his wife. He is a peculiar man, but one of the noblest in the world."[29]

"She has had enough flattery to turn any ordinary woman silly," one newspaper quoted a reported Cleveland intimate, "but that has not affected her a particle, and you will find that she is just the woman to show all kinds of thoughtful little courtesies to the family who will succeed her at the white house. Really, she feels the defeat more for the president's ambitions than for her own sake."[30]

Frances was again compared with some of the nation's most popular presidential wives:

> The long line of women who have presided as hostesses at the white house have had new lustre thrown about the position by the graceful girl who was the first and only one among presidents' wives to celebrate her wedding in the historic mansion. She will be ranked in coming time with Mrs. Madison and Miss Harriet Lane as one of the three most popular women who have held the position.
>
> Side by side with the queenly Martha Washington's portrait should hang that of Frances Folsom Cleveland, the sweet girl-wife of the twenty-second president of the United States.[31]

Frances, on the other hand, was not quite ready to be dismissed permanently from the Washington scene. As she and the president prepared to leave the White House, she turned to one of the stewards and said, "Now, Jerry, I want you to take good care of all the furniture and ornaments in the house, and not let any of them get lost or broken, for I want to find everything just as it is now, when we come back again."

The somewhat baffled Jerry asked Frances when she expected that return to be. "We are coming back just four years from today."[32]

# 6

# "Life is very smooth and even and beautiful"

Well-wishers cheered the Clevelands' train as it pulled into the station in northern New Jersey on the evening following Harrison's inauguration. After a dinner with friends, the couple was ferried to New York and driven to their apartments in the Victoria Hotel, in Manhattan. Daniel Lamont, continuing in his role of factotum to the couple, stayed behind to see the safe shipment of Frank's St. Bernard, Kay, to friends on Long Island, who had agreed to care for her pet.

Frank's friend, Katherine Willard, assumed that Frank deftly slid into her new, private life as easily as she had taken on the role of first lady.

> My dear Francesca,
>
> I am hoping that you accomplished your departure from Washington without too great fatigue or other serious results. Probably this afternoon you are sitting at your Fifth Avenue window, "surveying the surging mass of humanity below." I say probably, knowing full well that in reality—you're not yet out of church and you attended some service this morning.[1]

However, Frank's classmate from Wells, Minnie Alexander, expressed her concern for Frank's mental, emotional, and physical well-being.

My dearest Pippa:
    I wonder what you are doing this beautiful Sabbath—;
—and how often I have wondered if the "tired body," "the tired mind," and "the tired heart" are getting rested.

Minnie offers Frank solace in the subsequent lines of her letter:

> So tired, hard-but-not-too-tired
> To place my hand in Thine,
> To lay my head upon Thy breast,
> And know Thy love is mine.[2]

    Frank was tired, and the transition from new bride and president's wife to private life was not as easy as many of Frank's close circle assumed. Helena Gilder encouraged Frank to get some rest, as did other friends who had established correspondence with Frank over the previous two years.

    On the other hand, Emma had little sympathy for the adjustments her daughter faced, and she was uncharacteristically critical. "This will be an opportunity to see if you can run a household by yourself," Emma Folsom wrote in a letter that was noticeably caustic in tone.

    It was not the first time there had been hints of tension between the two women. Gilder had commented on an exchange he had witnessed between the mother and daughter, prompting an apologetic reply from Frank: "I appreciate what you say of my mother—My Laureate—and I like you better that you say it. My wonder is that I am better with such a mother—I hope you did not think I spoke too sharply to her that afternoon. When she proposed our not going to 103 E. 15th—I didn't mean to be cross with her—or disrespectful—but I knew her suggestion was not her own wish or thought. It is always hard enough to remember being *sharp* to those we love, but it's worse when it happened before others we love."[3]

    Some of the most recent change in the relationship was prompted by Emma's marriage to an old friend from Buffalo, and distant cousin, Henry Perrine. Cleveland reported the event in a letter to a friend:

> I am entirely alone tonight and that leads me to say that
> this condition comes from the marriage of Mrs. Folsom,

which I expect took place tonight. It came off a little
sooner than we expected it would. She had our consent
to be married in June but she went to Jackson, Mich.,
with the man there and the young things got in a hurry.
Things are getting into a pretty tough condition when
a man can't keep his mother-in-law in the traces. Mrs.
Cleveland started last night to see the show.

. . . I am rather sorry to let Mrs. Folsom go, but of
course there was nothing to be said. And she will live in
Buffalo—the place I hate above all others.[4]

Shortly after the marriage, a series of demanding and difficult
letters began arriving from Emma. "Why hasn't Lena [Frank's maid]
sent my corsets?" Emma asked in one letter. In another, Emma wrote,
"I attended a new church, and I was afraid people would stare at me,
but I got through it." She noted that she had received a golden hair-
piece as a wedding gift from a neighbor, "like the one the President
gave you, but smaller." There were no anniversary wishes in this letter,
dated on the third anniversary of the Clevelands' marriage.[5]

Emma chided Frank about the frequency of her correspondence: "I would mildly suggest that you have your letters mailed
more promptly for I think you must have written some before
Saturday. . . . Cornie [Emma's stepdaughter] thinks . . . if it were not
for my *new* daughter who is *never* neglectful of me, I would really
be an object of pity. . . ."

Later in the same letter, Emma writes, "Would you think me
being ungrateful if I should ask if you would be willing to change
the after dinner coffee cups you sent me? They hold so little—only
half what an ordinary after dinner coffee cup holds—that I do not
like to offer anyone so little coffee. They are *very* pretty but not
exactly practical. . . ."

As if to soften what has otherwise been a scolding tone, Emma
concludes: "I miss you so much I hoped you might feel so strong a
desire to see me in my new home."[6]

Frank was concerned for her mother's happiness and her social
acceptance in Buffalo. Shortly after returning from Emma's wedding,
Frank wrote to Cora Townsend, the mother of her former fiancé,
Charles Townsend, who had broadcast the news of Frank's engagement

after reading the letter to the family. The family's gossip unleashed the intense newspaper coverage and intrusion into Frank's and the president's pre-nuptial privacy.

Frank's angry response at the disclosure of her engagement was to cease communication with the family. Now, with Emma's return to Buffalo, mending fences was essential for Emma's reentry into Buffalo society.

"I received your letter three years ago [this would have been at the time of Frank's wedding] and didn't answer. I ask your forgiveness . . . and ask for the matter to be dropped and for our friendship to be renewed," Frank wrote. She signed herself "Frank," and not the formal "Frances F. Cleveland" that she used in her nonpersonal letters. At the end of the letter, Frank encourages the Townsends to visit Emma "in her new home in Buffalo."[7]

Mrs. Townsend accepted Frank's peace offering, but not without blaming Frank for the reason the secret was revealed in the first place. Mrs. Townsend also hints that Frank's motivation for writing was not wholly altruistic, but was prompted by her mother's marriage to Henry Perrine, although the woman does ultimately give Frank the benefit of the doubt.

> My dear Frank,
>
> Three years is a long time to have a letter remain unanswered that was sent in the trust of genuine friendship and with feelings of affectionate pride, with never a suspicion that it will be perceived in any other way for my conscience was so clear of offense, and I am sure that the hurt that you felt could not have been greater than mine. When you were so willing to sunder your friendship with us all for a mistake which could have been avoided, had I been prepared for the secret your letter contained by the word of secrecy being given at the beginning rather [than at] the ending of the letter, for nothing is more natural in our family than to read foreign letters aloud. But your letter of May 26 assures me that what then seemed inexcusable seems natural to you now, and that you desire our friendship may begin where it left off.

Had Cornie [Perrine] not told me of a conversation she had with you last winter, I should regret to feel that Mr. Perrine's marriage with your mother was the cause of your writing as you have to me, but I do believe, my dear Frank, that you are sincere in your old feeling for me in wishing the past to be forgotten. We will have it so, and I shall take pleasure in calling upon your mother, and trust the future will bring us again together in the old way and your wish shall be respected and it is mine as well that the affair may never be referred to again. . . .

Believe me very sincerely and lovingly your friend,
Mrs. R. Townsend[8]

Cleveland's prodigious work habits did not change with the end of the presidency. In the two years following his marriage, Cleveland had repeatedly asserted in letters to friends and in public interviews that he wanted to "live with his wife as other men live with their wives." In reality, Cleveland continued to be a "man's man," with his time divided among his work, his duck hunting, and his fishing. Frank was given whatever time remained.

In an interview with newspaper journalists shortly before leaving the White House, Frank expressed her wish to travel to Europe with the president and get away from the demands and pressures that had been their common life in Washington. "She would prefer to go abroad, spend six months or more in quiet travel and sightseeing, and then return to New York and settle down to housekeeping in a home of her own."[9]

Cleveland, however, did not believe that he would be able to travel quietly anywhere, and was especially averse to sea travel. The one person who obviously understood him was his sister, Rose, who observed: "Work is so much of my brother's life that he would not thrive without his daily systematic toil."[10]

Cleveland took a position in the law firm of Francis Lynde Stetson, the attorney who represented the tycoon J. P. Morgan. Cleveland's work cast him more in the role of a mediator than of a practicing attorney. Nonetheless, he brought his tremendous energies and attention to detail to bear on his position, and also became better known among the tycoons of the Gilded Age. Cleveland's access to New York's "select four hundred" may have opened social doors for Frank, but her own adeptness and skill made her a natural for entrée into the nation's highest social circles.

In response, Frank followed the pattern typical of most upper-class marriages of the day and created a life of her own within the framework that Cleveland found acceptable. She devoted herself to charity work and patronizing the arts. In rare instances, the Clevelands socialized together, attending dinners for friends, or, on the rarest of occasions, serving on a committee together. Gilder was successful in securing Frank's, Emma's, and Cleveland's participation on the Executive Committee for an exhibition of paintings of George Washington: "Father of his Country, his Generals, his family and his contemporaries charged with the affairs of state."[11]

The extent of the separateness of their lives is revealed in a letter that Frank wrote to Helena Gilder in mid-May, two days before Emma's marriage.

> My dear Helena,
>     My husband has invited me to drive with him this afternoon for the first time since we came to New York—and I hadn't the heart to refuse—or to even tell him I had another plan. We can see the pictures some other time, can't we? I don't see enough of my husband to be willing to miss such a chance.[12]

Frank did not attend the 1889 Wells College commencement ceremonies. She and Cleveland had been invited to Wells to lay a cornerstone in the newly erected building that replaced Morgan Hall, which had been gutted by fire two years after Frank's graduation. As a trustee, the former first lady of the nation, and an alumna of the school, her presence was eagerly sought.

Instead, Frank left New York City for the Gilder cottage, in Marion, in early June. Her withdrawal from New York life and the tone of Cleveland's letters suggest that Frank was exhibiting the same hurt and anger—what we would term today "depression"—that others had seen in her at the time she withdrew from high school in 1881. The stakes were higher now. She could not leave her marriage, but she could withdraw from daily contact with her husband. The Gilders' cottage in Marion offered just that type of refuge.

Cleveland's letters during that time carry a plaintive tone. There is a hint that Frank needed reassurance from him, while she was, at the same time, distancing herself from him by staying with the Gilders. Cleveland typically worked Monday through Thursday, and took a train to Marion to join Frank for a long weekend. With multiple daily mail deliveries, it was common for the couple to write to and receive from each other several letters daily. A typical letter from Cleveland read: "Dr. Van Dyck called last night, and I think will write to you . . . love to the Gilders. . . . I like my rooms . . . and I had a good night's sleep last night. . . . With all the love there is in human hearts and with love to the Gilders. Your devoted husband, Grover Cleveland."[13]

A week later, he wrote again about how much he missed her and how much happiness she had given him. He also expressed his pleasure at seeing her again over the weekend.[14]

His short notes typically detailed his daily activities—the time he arrived in the office, where and what he ate for dinner, the time he went to bed. His letter of June 12 conveyed an anxiousness about their separation and his desire to see her again on the weekend. Two days later, he wrote, "I love you dearly and want to see you very much. I must go fishing *a little* but will spend most of my time with you, I hope. I don't see how I can stay with you longer than Monday evening, because I have partly agreed to go a-fishing next Thursday."[15]

Frank, in turn, looked for comfort from her close friends from Wells. She extended an invitation to Minnie to visit in Marion, but Minnie had family obligations and could not make the trip. "My dear," she wrote to Frank, "can I tell you how glad your letter made me in that it said, 'Come to me.' A great throb of joy came to me that you should want me—just such throbs as make the heart glad as sorrow makes it ache. That you wanted me the least bit took away a part of my disappointment in not being able to go to you."[16]

Katherine Willard spent time with her at Marion in late August, but the visit did not go well for the two friends. In a letter written shortly after the visit's end, Katherine wrote at length about the changes she observed in Frank. In a subsequent letter, Katherine expressed her jealousy of Frank's relationships with the Gilders, their family, and their circle of friends in Marion. Katherine referred to herself as a "misfit" in the group, although her vocal training and interest in the arts would suggest that she was a natural addition to the writers, painters, and actors that composed the Gilders' inner circle:

> Perhaps at Marion affairs were strained: truthfully, I felt that they were and that I should not care to repeat the experience but I have gotten back to where I think of you quite as you seemed to me always before. At Marion I thought you more changed than I had ever known you before and I was disappointed, but I fancy 'twas not in yourself at all—simply some outside influence which I did not understand and which did not please me. In most combinations I think you would not lose at all but there could be situations where I should prefer to reflect upon my heart's image of you than to be with you—not for your sake, Francesca, but my own, and hereafter I should always know how to avoid such a situation. . . .[17]

Frank's response soothes Katherine's anger and anxieties. A week later, she wrote Frank: "Tonight I have only time to thank you for your blessed letter which came this afternoon, and to tell you that it was cruel to lay upon you what probably belonged to me—the general misfit of affairs at Marion. . . ."[18]

The close friendship between Gilder and Frank grew during that summer. Gilder was an inveterate optimist, a romantic in his outlook on life. Those who knew the Gilders characterized them as "genteel": passionate in their feelings and warm in their friendships.[19]

When the offices of the *Century Magazine* burned, destroying much of his life's work, Gilder took the tragedy in stride, as Frank noted in a letter to him.

> My heart stood still until I read that the long poem was saved. But what a freak of chance to burn the box and save the contents. Why wasn't it the *company* that lost the most? But no it must be you—you of all people—you who care so much for the tiniest thing that belongs to

you. And yet you are so outwardly cheerful—and so glad it isn't any worse than it is!!

A certain lady I have met has one saving trait—she says "I say Richard Gilder—the only perfect man I know." I think poor Helena will be distressed. I only hope it won't plunge her into the blues again. Go up there as soon as you can and get a rest I know you do need it—and please really rest . . .

We are full of sympathy and exasperation from the President to Mary and Lena—and all send messages full of the same [sympathy and exasperation].

Faithfully,

F.F.C.[20]

Gilder used his poetry to express his innermost thoughts, and to encourage his friends. One poem, written during Frank's difficult summer, expresses his care for her, along with a cautionary note that the two were to be circumspect in their behavior toward each other.

August 1889
Song

I.

I care not if the skies are white
    Nor if the fields are gold;
I care not whether tis dark or bright
    Or winds blow soft, or cold—
    But Oh the dark, dark woods
    For thee, and me, and love.

II.

Let all but one at last depart—
    The great would say farewell:
This is the kingdom of the heart
    Where only two may dwell.
    And Oh the deep, deep woods,
    For thee, and me, and love.

R.W.G.[21]

Gilder added as a postscript: "Sow thou sorrow—and thou shalt keep it; Sow thou joy—and thou shalt reap it."[22]

Gilder had a reputation for taking on causes, and one to which he devoted a considerable amount of energy was the establishment of free kindergartens in New York City. He founded the New York Kindergarten Association, and served as its president. Frank was the first vice president, and the two worked together to promote the importance of kindergarten programs.

The idea of the kindergarten was developed by Friedrich Froebel, a German educator, in the 1850s. His educational experiments in his home country proved to him that children as young as four or five years of age benefited from organized classes that taught them movement, basic colors and shapes, and behavior. Frank had attended a private kindergarten in Buffalo as a young girl, and now she became active in the efforts to promote free kindergartens as an agent of social change for impoverished, and often immigrant, children in the United States.

The New York Kindergarten Association (NYKA) was one of many organizations formed nationwide in response to the lack of interest in kindergarten on the part of the country's already established public school system. "Another group of people, frustrated at the lack of interest by the public schools, turned to organizing free kindergarten associations to support charity kindergartens for children of the poor. These people hoped that free kindergartens would give the slum child a chance he would not otherwise have to enable him to rise above the disadvantages of poverty and neglect."[23]

This was the view espoused by the leaders of the NYKA. "Plant a free kindergarten in any quarter of this overcrowded metropolis, and you have begun then and there the work of making better lives, better homes, better citizens, and a better city," was a statement of Richard Watson Gilder's that was frequently quoted in support of the establishment of free kindergartens.[24]

The efforts to establish the programs were not glamorous. Kindergartens were most frequently located in the most congested areas of New York, because they served the immigrant and poor families packed into New York's tenements. Gilder challenged the school officials of New York, who were initially opposed to establishing kindergartens as part of the public school structure. The *Critic* remarked, "The kindergarten method of instruction, he said, is no longer an experiment, but a practical and established success. Why was it, then, that in the list of fifty cities of the United States that have at least one kindergarten in connection with their system of public instruction, the name of New York did not appear? Why was it that St. Louis, Boston, Philadelphia and Milwaukee had established the system on a large scale in connection with their public schools, while New York is only beginning to inquire into the matter?"[25]

The NYKA initially established two free kindergartens, one located at East Fifty-third Street, and a second at East Sixty-second Street under the auspices of the alumnae of the New York Normal College. Frank's presence at a fund-raising fair for the college's kindergarten was said to have increased overall attendance and giving. "Mrs. Cleveland was one of the patronesses of the fair. . . . [She] visited each booth and complimented the numerous attractive features of the fair very warmly."[26]

However, Frank's major efforts were directed toward the Fifty-third Street Kindergarten, which had to turn away applicants and gave preference to the poorest children. For the Christmas of 1890, she and Mrs. George H. Putnam (the wife of the founder of the publishing firm G. H. Putnam and Sons) provided a Christmas tree "loaded with toys, popcorn and other delights." Frank assisted in the distribution of gifts to the children. It is highly likely that she was instrumental in R. H. Macy & Company donating $500 worth of clothing to the kindergarten's children, a significant sum for the time.[27]

That same Christmas, Frank dressed a doll that was donated to a charity doll show and auction. Her doll, dubbed a "belle in evening toilet," brought $115. A portion of the proceeds were given to the Fifty-third Street Kindergarten, "Mrs. Cleveland's protegés."[28]

Frank was active in other charity work, as well. She laid a cornerstone for a new building for the New York Eye and Ear Hospital. She sold roses at a benefit for poor immigrant girls organized by the Mission of Our Lady of the Rosary. Her popularity was still so high that the majority of the crowd wanted to purchase its roses from her, which required that a line form so that everyone who wanted to could buy a flower. An article announcing the event had noted that Frank would be attending the event with Cleveland, but, as was often the case, he was not present.[29]

Theatrical events were another means of fund-raising. By early 1891, Frank had been able to recruit several of New York's most prominent socialites to the list of supporters for the NYKA. Her friend Flora Whitney joined the cause, as did Mrs. Andrew Carnegie and Mrs. Cornelius Vanderbilt.[30]

Frank's social and charitable activities formed the nexus of her New York life. In addition to her close relationship with the Gilders, Frank maintained her friendships with Flora Whitney and Mrs. Daniel Lamont. She added the Whitneys' daughter, Susan Dimosch, and the Andrew Carnegies to her inner circle.

In 1890, the Clevelands purchased Gray Gables, a summer home in Buzzards Bay, Massachusetts, near Marion. Unlike their New York apartments, which never had the feel of home for Frank, Gray Gables was Frank's first real home since the death of her father. It afforded Cleveland the opportunity to fish to his heart's content and return home to his wife at the end of the day.

Gray Gables was a large, sprawling home with a wide verandah, wood siding, and a rustic appearance. With the waterfront on one side and the seclusion of pine trees around the rest of the house, the Clevelands enjoyed the privacy and quiet they both craved.

While Cleveland continued to work in the city during the summertime, his schedule shows that he increasingly extended his time at Gray Gables. The couple also shared social contacts, notably the Gilders and the Joseph Jeffersons, and their extended circle of friends. (Joseph Jefferson was a prominent actor of the day, and he and his wife had a home in Marion.) For the first time in over a year, Frank's letters contain a hint of satisfaction:

> Dearest Helena,
> . . . I am growing tired of city life (I've been back just a week!). It seems so dreadful to be unable to step out on the ground—the earth itself—not stones and pavements. I feel now as if nothing the city gives could ever make up for all that. I had such a beautiful summer you see.[31]

More change was in the air for Frank. Sometime in the early spring of 1891, she realized that she was pregnant. Although there had been suggestions in newspaper gossip columns of a pregnancy earlier in the couple's marriage, there is no indication that Frank had been expecting previously and had suffered a miscarriage.

Pregnancy was not discussed openly in the 1890s, and so Frank uses the accepted euphemisms of the day to describe her condition. "I am very well—aside from occasionally getting too tired—not inside tired—mostly my head because I know I must be careful," she wrote Helena at the end of May from Gray Gables.[32]

Again, toward the end of her term, she assures Helena (who has had three children):

> Dearest Helena,
>
> You are so good to think so much about me that I truly feel sort of guilty that I do not deserve more sympathy—but I am so well and so cheerful that it really seems I ought to turn about and look after you. I am greatly distressed by what you write of your own condition.
>
> . . . So many pretty things are coming every day. I have just stopped to open a box from Buffalo and I find a dainty white silk cover with finest *babiest* lace. Everybody is kind—and I hear from people in such a sweet way who surprise me greatly to think they have remembered me. They say all the world loves a lover—I should say all the world loves a baby.[33]

Ruth Cleveland was born on October 3, 1891. Her arrival evoked a visceral response in her fifty-four-year-old father, and a more typical maternal response on the part of her twenty-seven-year-old mother.

Cleveland's friend and contemporary, Wilson Bissell, had also married a much younger woman, who was now expecting a child. Cleveland, in an effort to convey his own emotional response to the birth of his daughter, wrote:

> October 21, 1891
>
> The house is perfectly quiet—at ten o'clock. I have just been up to find my wife and child sleeping and the nurse too. Only our mother-in-law is awake.
>
> I feel an impulse to write to you. And I feel too that unless I make an effort, I shall write in a strange fashion

to you. I, who have just entered the real world, and see in a small child more of value than I have ever called my own before; who puts aside, as hardly worth a thought, all that has gone before—fame, honor, place, everything—reach out my hand to you and fervently express the wish—the best my great friendship for you yields—that in safety and in joy you may soon reach my estate.

I think a great deal about you and your dear wife just now. I think a little of your anxiety and suspense, a little of the cloud that must pass over her, but a great deal of the joy and happiness that will come to both of you when anxiety and suspense are over and the cloud is past.

Give our love to Mrs. Bissell, and let me know when you are made happy.[34]

Emma wrote a note to Helena Gilder two days after Ruth's birth:

Oct. 5, 1891
My dear Mrs. Gilder,
I know you will like to hear . . . how Frank is getting on, and I am so happy to be able to tell you that she and the precious little Ruth are both doing nicely. It was rather a long labor with Frank—but not at all severe and she was able to watch the first dressing of the baby with as much interest as any of us. She does not look as if anything had happened and is far from being "the pale mother" you have imagined. That baby is very pretty—strong and [healthy]—so says not only grandmamma, but everyone who has seen her. She has dark brown hair and dark eyes. . . .[35]

Within two months, Frank had traveled with the baby to the Clevelands' cottage at Lakewood, New Jersey. Although the Clevelands hired a nurse to take care of their daughter, Frank was an unusually attentive mother for her social class. She bathed Ruth daily and scheduled her activities to accommodate her daughter's needs. However, motherhood did not diminish Frances's charitable interests, and she remained involved in her activities, particularly anything regarding the kindergartens.

Frances was also responsive to Cleveland's needs, as is evident from a letter that she wrote to Helena Gilder. He was apparently impatient with the demands of an infant, whether as a result of his age or from years of being away from young children. Frances made an effort to accommodate him.

Dec. 6, 1891
Lakewood, NJ
I am ready now to grow strong and very fat, with a good appetite and a throat capable of carrying down what food Miss Ruth and I need and desire. I think it is agreeing with her beautifully although I am sure my sore throat depressed her a little. The weather is so mild she can be out two or three or even four hours and I drive in the morning and walk in the PM.

We made the journey very comfortably—bodily— though I was "in a state" as every body was out and looking and listening for the baby to cry. Alone I would not have cared. She might have been *yelling* all the way but we are different. I suspect G.C. would have been disgusted if she had not been the [very] good girl she was. The station was crowded with staring people—evidently bound to have a glimpse of the young lady—and one woman pushed up to Annie [the Cleveland's nurse] and demanded to see her. Annie told her the baby was not on exhibition. I think I have a treasure in Annie.[36]

Frances also found herself accommodating Cleveland's wishes with regard to any activities that might put her in a public light, as evident from what she wrote to Helena: "Will you please give R[ichard Gilder] the enclosed paper? The President seems to prefer I should not sign the petition. I can't see the harm myself and should be glad to do so, but he is a little set in his ideas of what women should and should not do in public matters—I signed the Kindergarten thanks."

Frank closes with this word of encouragement to Helena Gilder: "Your Mrs. Von Slosch [?] did splendidly for the Kindergarten—but

I think you did more[.] It is easy to get up and say things you have been working to say for years—our writing mindless tiresome notes when you aren't well is another matter."[37]

Frank's interest in the establishment of kindergartens did not lessen with Ruth's birth. In a letter to Richard Gilder, Frank asks for ideas regarding the purchase of a Christmas gift for Helena. She suggests a muff, then adds, "How about Christmas for the Kindergartens?—If we could be in town just for those things—but we are so happy here and so well. I am trying to think of what book G.C. wants."[38]

A few days later, she wrote to Helena: "Don't I wish I could go in for the 14th—but you know how these babies are. They must eat—or drink rather. Ruth weighs by the way 12 lbs 7½ oz. She has gained 12½ oz in one week and she is a dumpling. I don't know what I have gained—except contentment and happiness resulting—and that is everything. Life is very smooth and even and beautiful."[39]

# 7

# "Mrs. Cleveland knew what she wanted"

Between the years 1888 and 1892, Frances's civic and philanthropic work kept her in the public eye. Her position as vice president of the New York Kindergarten Association enabled her to develop contacts with other affluent women in New York and nationwide who promoted the work of the kindergartens. Frances continued to serve as president of the Eastern Association of Wells College, although she complained to Helena Gilder that she wished that that group would elect another leader. Frances also lent her name and her support to various artistic, literary, and musical endeavors, seeking to strengthen the arts in New York City and environs.

Her popularity had diminished little since she had left the White House in March 1889, and it was common for the *New York Times* to report on her activities at least twice a month. The press coverage, and the connections forged by Frances's activities, built political support for Cleveland among the New York Four Hundred. This group was considered the most influential in the country in the realm of finance, the arts, and, of course, politics.

Flora Payne Whitney had played a large role in Frances's introduction into the elite of New York society. The Clevelands' deepening friendship with the Gilders was another social and political plus. As editor of the highly influential *Century Magazine*, Gilder could be counted on to pull in other Republican supporters, as well as to give Cleveland favorable press coverage. Cleveland's own work in the Stetson law firm built a rapport with J. P. Morgan, Commodore E. C. Benedict, and other New York Republicans.

The Clevelands' combined efforts generated sufficient Republican support to help Cleveland recapture the majority of New York's votes in the 1892 election. As mentioned, four years earlier Harrison had carried the state and its electoral votes had won him the presidency, even though Cleveland had won the majority of the popular vote nationwide.

Cleveland refused to acknowledge the political value of his wife's activities, and discouraged her participation in things he did not appreciate. Frances complained about Cleveland's attitude in a letter to Helena Gilder, while acknowledging she would have to acquiesce to his wishes, if only to keep things peaceful between them: "Then New York is never very satisfactory to me because the President is never satisfied if I am doing anything he does not appreciate. [He does not appreciate] that many things interest me which would bore him—things which he isn't obliged to do himself—but which it worries him to have me do because they would bore him if he had to do them. This thing for Saturday is exactly one of the sort of things I mean. I want his winter to be as easy for him in every way as is possible."[1]

Newspaper journalists, on the other hand, fully appreciated Frances's contributions to Cleveland's political fortunes, and wrote glowingly of her return to the White House.

> New York society certainly has, on selfish grounds, every reason to be glad of the change in the Administration which the result of Tuesday will bring about [wrote the *New York Times* society columnist a few days after the 1892 election].
>
> There is a growing interest felt in political matters among the members of the fashionable world, and a growing appreciation of the social side of the Administration at Washington. . . . Mr. and Mrs. Cleveland have now been residents of New York for some years, and have gone more into society than their predecessors, while Mrs. Whitney's position in New York and her close and friendly relations with the Clevelands have added in producing an unusual amount of interest in Mr. Cleveland's recent candidacy and

of a general desire that he and his charming young wife should once more occupy the White House.[2]

However, Frances's priorities had changed. Although she had ample household help, including a full-time nurse for Ruth, Frances selected her activities and organized her schedule with greater attention to the demands of her daughter and husband. She wrote to Helena Gilder:

> GC will undoubtedly spend the rest of this week at the club—and I shall not think of going back [to Manhattan] before he does. Ruth is so much better off here where she can be constantly out of doors and naturally I am better where there is not pulling and hauling in forty directions at one time. . . . They are making some very good alterations and I think it would be much better for GC to have the amount of rest he can get only here before he goes to Washington. It will leave us a little time in New York.
>
> There is so much I counted on doing this winter but I cannot have everything and health for my husband naturally comes first.[3]

As they had during their first administration, the Clevelands looked for a home where they could retreat from the White House once the formal social season had ended. Having sold Oak View following their move from Washington in 1889, they rented a house on Woodley Road. Renovations to the house included cutting a doorway into the bathroom on the second floor and adding a bathroom on the "principal floor." The house was to have entirely new plumbing installed, as well as an artesian well dug to ensure the safety of the drinking water.

Although the lease on the house was intended for one year only, the extensive renovations were estimated to cost between $4,000 and $5,000. The property manager, Edward J. Stellwagen, wrote to the Clevelands' agent, "As the entire internal arrangement of the house will be changed, by the alterations which will be made in the spring of /94, whatever is done now, by way of painting and papering, will be simply work which will then be destroyed. I am therefore anxious that no very expensive paper should be used, and hope Mrs. Cleveland may find in the cheaper priced papers patterns which will please her."[4]

Many of the Clevelands' closest confidantes were returning to Washington with them. The Lamonts would be a part of their inner circle, and Cleveland's close friend from his Buffalo days, Wilson Bissell, had accepted the position of postmaster general. Bissell had followed his friend's example and married a much younger woman in 1890. Mrs. Bissell, like Frank's friend Katherine Willard, had studied music in Germany and embarked on a vocal career prior to her marriage. The two women had much in common in their interests and husbands. The Bissells' daughter, Margaret, was born just a few days after Ruth Cleveland. Frances's namesake, Frances Lamont, and Margaret Bissell became Ruth Cleveland's playmates and attended the White House kindergarten that Frances organized when the girls became old enough to attend.

Absent from her circle this time would be Flora Payne Whitney, the doyenne of Washington social life during the first Cleveland years, and Frances's mentor in navigating both the capital's and New York's labyrinthine social structures. Mrs. Whitney had died unexpectedly just a month before the inauguration. One of her last social activities, at the end of January, was to host a reception for Frances.

March 4, 1893, inauguration day, was bitterly cold. Snow fell in the morning, and there were concerns about the carriages being able to negotiate the snow-covered Washington streets. The family had spent the previous night in Arlington House, preparing to retake the White House at noon, when Cleveland would be sworn in as president for a second time.

The public had high expectations. The male electorate hoped that Cleveland's honesty and courage would pull the nation out of its severe economic depression. Women saw Frances as the dazzling star in the administration's social crown. This time, she came to Washington not as the inexperienced schoolgirl, but as a married woman and as a mother. Her initial White House years as an ingenue first lady were now augmented by four years spent in New York's society and charity circles.

"Mrs. Cleveland's return will be to society like the opening of a familiar book at a favorite chapter . . . ," enthused the *New York Times*. "The wife who came to preside in the White House nearly seven years ago, and who returns now a young matron with the added dignity of motherhood, has in all circumstances conducted herself with becoming dignity and discretion."[5]

In the 1800s, participation in the inauguration was a strictly masculine affair. When the carriage came to Arlington House to pick up the president-elect to take him to the White House, where he would join President Harrison for the ride to the inauguration, Cleveland bade farewell to the officials and personal friends who had gathered to see him. Frances "called him back, and, with utter disregard for the assembled company, threw her arms about her husband and kissed him several times, bidding him 'godspeed' on his way to take the oath of office."[6]

As Washington officialdom witnessed the orderly transfer of presidential power, Frances reassumed her power as first lady away from the direct glare of the public eye. Irwin H. (Ike) Hoover, who had been hired as a steward during the Harrison administration, was a young man at the time.

> White House employes have no politics and were immune to political overturns even in the days when "to the victors belong the spoils" was the rule [Hoover wrote in his memoirs]. Only once has the staff been swept out with a change of administration, and this was on the return of the Clevelands. Many incumbents have dreamed of regaining the White House, but only the Clevelands did. This was the explanation. The changes were personal rather than political. It seemed that the Harrisons had gradually dropped many of the staff they had inherited from the Cleveland first term. At noon of March 4, 1893, in marched the old Cleveland steward with his own corps, and the ax fell. Of the domestic staff, Miss Josephine Kniep, the housekeeper, alone escaped, and within a month I was the only survivor downstairs. It was well for me that electricity still was a novelty, or I should have had two years rather than forty-two in the White House to remember.[7]

Hoover soon learned that while Mrs. Cleveland was kind and gracious, she also had definite opinions. "Mrs. Cleveland knew what she wanted, and we saw more changes in the first week of her return than the oldest hand could remember. Not until the Tafts came did I see its like again. This was something more than the normal disposition of a woman to move a chair anywhere but where her predecessor has left it."[8]

The Clevelands quickly settled into their typical routine. They ate breakfast together at nine o'clock. Lunch was at one-thirty, and dinner was served at seven-thirty. Frances was fanatical about making sure that she and the president had a daily drive around four o'clock. Only a cabinet meeting preempted this ritual, but there were times when the business of government did not deter her from trying, usually futilely, to pry Cleveland away from his duties.

In recounting his years in the second Cleveland administration, the secretary of the navy Hilary Herbert told the story of the time Frances came into Cleveland's office while Cleveland and he were meeting:

> One bright afternoon I was sitting with the President going over some business [Herbert recollected]. The hour for his usual afternoon drive had arrived. Mrs. Cleveland came in dressed for the ride, gauntlets in hand. "Well," she said, addressing herself to the President, "it's time for you to go." "I can't go this evening," was the reply, "Secretary Herbert has some business he wants to talk over with me." "Yes," she said, tapping him at the same time playfully on the knee with one of her gauntlets, "that's always the way. You prefer your Secretaries to me," and then turning to me she said, "I hate every one of you cabinet officers. You are always taking him when you know that he needs his drive." But the business went on.[9]

Her birds and dogs once again graced the White House, including three pedigreed dachshunds shipped to Frances directly from Germany in September.[10]

Frank continued to show her interest in the establishment of free kindergartens. She attended a lecture given by Mrs. Virginia T. Smith, who had been successful in introducing kindergartens into the public school system in Connecticut. Frank had worked with the NYKA in the hope of achieving a similar result.[11]

Emma Perrine had joined the crusade on behalf of the establishment of kindergartens. "I still have about two hundred dollars to raise for our kindergarten, and am now engaged in the delightful task of getting up an entertainment for it," she wrote Frances.[12]

Mother and daughter had reconciled at some point following Frank's departure from the White House four years earlier. "You *are* the dearest child in the world, and your sweet letter has given me many pleasant things to think of although it *did* bring the tears to my eyes, darling little Ruth to think of her wanting to write Nomma a letter and associating your writing with me," wrote Emma in her opening. Emma approves Frank's decision to return to Dr. Sunderland's church, and demonstrates a new appreciation for the demands on Frank's time. "I received today a letter forwarded by you, a letter from an old schoolmate, at Phipps Union Seminary, who was in Washington March ninth and wrote to ask if she might call upon me. . . . May I tell her if she is still in W. she may call upon you? . . . I will send you her card . . . I will tell her of your Tuesdays and Fridays from 12–1."[13]

Privately, Frances expressed some misgivings about returning to the demands of public life. "Dearest," wrote Katherine Willard, "I have thought so often about your saying in your last letter that going back to Washington rather depressed you—that old things were neither their old selves nor yet anything new."[14]

However, Frank's sense of duty and commitment to her responsibilities overrode her innermost feelings. Once again, she was in the thick of behind-the-scenes politics. A letter from her friend Helen Fairchild Smith about a local postmaster position reveals Frank's knowledge of local politics and her involvement in patronage appointments when she knew the parties involved. "I am greatly surprised to hear what you write of Mr. Brown, I *know* nothing for I never heard a suspicion that he was not, or had not always been a 'Cleveland Democrat' . . . I certainly would not have written to Mrs. Bissell if I had supposed her political sympathies or her father's were with the Hill faction [Democrats opposed to Cleveland]."[15]

Another remnant from the first Cleveland administration also reared its ugly head: the use of Frances's image and name to sell products. A letter written to her in May 1893 by J. I. Connor questions why she presumably gave permission for her image and name to be used to promote a hair tonic, only to request that the use of her name be stopped.

> Dear Madam:
>
> To say the least, I am very much surprised at the contents of your letter, which just reached me. The last time I was at your house in Lakewood, if you remember, I asked if you would care if I used your picture to advertise the tonic, and you said, do not ask my permission but go on, and I hope you will make a fortune. Then I asked if you would be angry and you said you could not be—or you would tell me not to use it. I also asked if I could name it after you and you said there was a Cleveland Baking powder and you did not see why there could not be a Cleveland Hair Tonic. So I certainly thought you were perfectly satisfied.[16]

Both Frances and Cleveland protested strongly against the use of her name and image in advertising, without any success. Once again, Congress failed to take steps to protect her through legislation, believing that such a law would amount to a restriction of trade.

In early May, Frances revealed her pregnancy with her second child in a letter to Helena:

> . . . But I am really writing you on my own business. There is a new baby expected and I want you two to know it—no one else now—I have kept it all to myself probably nearly as long as I can. I mean as a *fact*. Rumors have counted for nothing for I don't believe any one has thought it a possibility—so late as the fall. March–April. May or June have been all I have heard. I told my mother a little while ago and if I had been near or with you I should have told you too but I haven't wanted to write it. It naturally doesn't now mean to me just what Ruth's expected coming did—but I know I am very well pleased and happy. I am perfectly and absolutely well. Better even than with Ruth and that is a blessing I know. I have so much else to do and think about that the time slips rapidly by.[17]

Frances indeed had much to think about, as she planned two back-to-back social events that demonstrated she was in top form as the leader of Washington society. On May 19, she and the president held a reception for the annual assembly of the Presbyterian Church. As had often been the case in the first administration, attendees would return to the end of the receiving line in the hope of having a second chance to greet Mrs. Cleveland. The *Washington Post* commented,

> The anxiety on the part of the visitors not only to greet Mrs. Cleveland, but to return to the East Room [the location of the reception] after they had made a tour of the White House, was so apparent that the men stationed at the various doorways to preserve order in the line of entrance and exit found their duties at times of no light nature. Every now and then some of the ladies, eluding the vigilance of the door-keepers, would manage to make their way back into the East Room where they stood as long as permitted to express in looks their admiration and the satisfaction they felt at their achievement.[18]

The highlight of the social season was the visit of the infanta Eulalia, the aunt of the king of Spain, and that nation's representative to the World's Fair, which was taking place in Chicago. The infanta paid a formal call on the president and Mrs. Cleveland on the morning of May 20, and Frances returned the call in the afternoon. Cleveland did not accompany his wife for the afternoon visit, although all of Washington was curious to see if he would do so. Instead, he followed a protocol that had been established the previous month when the Hawaiian queen, Kapiolani, had visited. Colonel John M. Wilson, U.S. Army, accompanied Frances, wearing his full military uniform.

The state dinner for the royal couple, held on May 23, featured a lavish menu and, as she had in the first administration, Frances served alcoholic beverages, while choosing not to drink them herself.

Little Neck Clams; Johannisberger Cabernet
Bisque of Crabs; Oloroso Apostoles, Vintage 1852
King of the Sea, Cucumber Salad; Chateau Mouton,
    Rothschild's Vintage, 1880.

Asparagus Points
Timbal of Pheasant, Truffle Sauce
Spring Lamb, New Peas. Champagne.
Fresh Mushrooms on Toast
Orange Romaine
Golden Plover; Lettuce and Tomato Salad. Burgundy Clos
   de Vougeot.

Following the meal, "individual creams, Charlotte Russe, assorted
cakes, strawberries, Cammembert [*sic*] and Roquefort cheese, coffee,
Spanish olives, radishes, candied fruit, almonds, Rosa Perfectos Cigars
and Liqueurs" were provided.[19]

The infanta's visit was considered the highlight of the spring
1893 social season. The pomp and pageantry captured the attention of the American public, and the event simultaneously masked
the deteriorating conditions of the nation's financial health and the
president's physical health.

In May, Cleveland discovered a rough place in his mouth, and he
immediately summoned a physician. Concern for the lesion prompted
his friend, Dr. Joseph Bryant, to order a biopsy of the tissue. The
sore was cancerous.

Within Cleveland's official family, the news came as a shock.
Daniel Lamont immediately expressed his dismay: "My God, sir, I
think the President is doomed!"[20]

Cleveland's reaction was political, as well as personal. America's
health was just as precarious as that of its president. The country
was on the brink of financial collapse. European bankers, who had
functioned as the de facto creditors of the United States by supply-
ing gold to the nation, had lost confidence in its economy. Railroads
were going bankrupt. Thousands of banks and businesses were failing.
When Cleveland took office in March, he found that Harrison had
depleted the U.S. Treasury by an estimated $100 million during his
four years in office.[21]

The public was pressuring Cleveland to call Congress into a
special session to consider repeal of the Sherman Silver Purchase Act
and to bring financial stability to the nation.

In no way was the nation to know that he needed surgery. "We
cannot risk any leak that would touch off a panic," Cleveland warned

his jittery medical team. "If rumor gets around that I am 'dying' then the country is dead, too. We must have secrecy."[22] With his characteristic loyalty and devotion to the Clevelands, Lamont assisted in the plans for the surgery.

By now, both Frances and the president were old hands at concealing their activities from the public eye. To read the press reports of the Clevelands' plans for the months of June, July, and August is like watching a perfectly choreographed pas de deux unfold on stage. The movements were masterfully designed, and the Clevelands' success at dissembling represented another outstanding performance demonstrating their deftness in the art of public deception.

On June 11, the *Washington Post* reported that "Mrs. Cleveland will leave the city in a fortnight to open the summer home at Buzzard's Bay, where she will spend a portion of the season, alternating between that resort and the country place on the Woodley road, of which she has so recently taken possession. Upon first moving into the latter place, President and Mrs. Cleveland had concluded to spend the entire summer there with the possible exception of August. . . . These plans have now, however, undergone a change, as Mrs. Cleveland is desirous of taking her little daughter to Buzzard's Bay before the advent of the intense heat in the city."[23] The very next day, the *New York Times* reprinted the same information.

The following week, both papers reported on the president's adoption of the "banting process," a diet fad of the day that assisted individuals in losing weight. It was not often that comments were made in the more respectable papers about the president's girth. This news, however, was a clever ruse to dispel any idea the public might have that the president's weight loss was due to illness.

The *New York Times* dismissed reports that the president was ill:

> Those imaginative persons who had put the President upon a "banting" programme, and who have been misinforming the public by giving the impression that the Chief Magistrate [*sic*] is invalided, would probably have lost respect for themselves as medical prophets if they could have seen the President today in the East Room while he was shaking hands with about 200 callers who were not frightened away by the erroneous reports of the extreme

hot weather. The President was looking as well as he has looked since he came here, and he received his callers cordially and cheerfully.[24]

The *Post* reported that the president would accompany Frances to Buzzards Bay, and then return to Washington.[25] The *Times* corrected this misconception, adding that "he wishes to close up a great deal of business that would have to be temporarily dropped if he went to Massachusetts now, and that he wants to keep on with his work until he can feel that he has earned the right to a Summer rest."[26]

Frances and Ruth arrived by train in New York on June 20, and then sailed up the sound with another coconspirator in the upcoming secret surgery. The Clevelands' friend Commodore E. C. Benedict transported the mother and daughter, and their attendants, to Buzzards Bay on his yacht, the *Oneida*. Another gentleman was seen with the pair, as Mrs. Cleveland headed toward the dock. The stranger refused to give his name to inquisitive reporters, but it is quite likely that this was one of the medical team who would assist in the president's upcoming surgery.[27]

The commodore's yacht was chosen as the site of the surgery.

Just over a week later, on June 30, the president left Washington, ostensibly for a fishing trip on the *Oneida*. On the same day, he issued a call for a special session of Congress to be convened on August 7. Questions arose about the president's health, and they were answered with statements about a flare-up of his rheumatism.

That night, Cleveland sat on the deck of the *Oneida*, smoking a cigar and becoming acquainted with Dr. Keen. Dr. Keen's concerns, as well as those of the others on the medical team—Dr. E. G. Janeway, of New York; Dr. O'Reilly; Dr. John P. Erdman; Dr. Bryant's assistant, Dr. Hasbrouck; and of course, Dr. Bryant—centered on how well Cleveland would handle sedation.[28]

There was no question that the surgery required that ether be administered to the president of the United States. The anesthetic was still relatively new, and monitoring the patient was something of a hit-or-miss proposition. Added to the typical concerns any physician has about operating on a patient, the physicians also considered the overall state of Cleveland's health. They suspected that he suffered from various undiagnosed, weight-related ailments. Dr. Keen, in his article, frankly described the president as "corpulent."[29]

The operation removed two of Cleveland's teeth, his entire upper left jaw, nearly up to the middle line of his mouth. A gelatinous substance was found inside Cleveland's mouth, and a subsequent biopsy confirmed that it was cancerous. There were no external incisions to betray the surgery.[30]

How much Frances understood of the severity of her husband's condition prior to the actual surgery will most likely never be known. In an age without secure communication, she could only guess at what was taking place on the *Oneida*. But just as she had acquitted herself so admirably seven years ago on the eve of her wedding, she again handled the press with her customary caution.

A week after Cleveland had boarded the *Oneida*, the press began to become suspicious of the president's absence from public view. Frances answered queries by saying that he was fine and was enjoying a fishing trip between New York and Buzzards Bay.

The *Washington Post*, tracking the president's whereabouts, reported on July 5 that the president had still not arrived at Buzzards Bay. The newspaper speculated that the *Oneida* was anchored somewhere between New London, Connecticut, and Buzzards Bay. Frances told members of the press that she thought "the President may spend two days more in fishing before reaching Gray Gables."[31]

Rumors started to fly that the president had cancer. "Stories of 'cancer' apparently are fictions, pure and simple," headlined a *Boston Globe* article, printed July 8, 1983.

> President Cleveland is not by any means the very sick man that has been written of since his arrival at Gray Gables. He is so far from being "laid up" that he was this afternoon planning to go fishing tomorrow. . . .
>
> Col. Lamont was asked this afternoon as to his observation on the improvement shown in the president's condition. The colonel said that the attack of rheumatism, while still somewhat troublesome, was yielding to the rest and quiet the president was enjoying.[32]

Lamont went on to say that the president's rheumatism had settled in his left knee and ankle, requiring Cleveland to wear a larger-sized shoe on the afflicted member. "When asked if there was any truth in the report that the president was suffering with a cancerous growth in the mouth, he replied that there was not," reported the *Globe*.[33]

Dr. Bryant offered the same denial. "Dr. Bryant said the president had been troubled with an aching tooth some time ago, and that it had been extracted, and that no operation whatever had been performed. When asked who had extracted the tooth and when it was, the doctor replied: 'O, it is a trivial matter.' "[34]

Reporters did not find it unusual that Cleveland was not speaking for himself. He had not yet been fitted with the rubber jaw that would enable him to speak clearly, and he limited his contact to his closest associates: his neighbor, Joseph Jefferson; Dr. Bryant; and Colonel Lamont.

The Clevelands' ordeal was not over. The president required a second operation on July 17, which was performed by Dr. Bryant on the *Oneida*.[35]

The *Globe* also reported that President Cleveland's sister, Mary Hoyt, had left her home near Omaha, Nebraska, to visit her brother because his "illness is more serious than is admitted by his physicians." Mrs. Hoyt told the press that she had "no intention of going east until she was called by a dispatch from Mrs. Cleveland."[36]

Following the second surgery, Cleveland was fitted with a vulcanized rubber jaw that gave him a normal appearance and allowed him to speak clearly.[37]

On July 20, the president spoke publicly for the first time in three weeks. "E.C. Benedict's steam yacht *Oneida*, having on board President Cleveland, Dr. Bryant, and the owner, dropped anchor late this afternoon. . . . A call at Gray Gables this evening found the President on the veranda. He expressed himself as having had a most enjoyable cruise and that he did not contemplate another during his stay here. In speaking of his physical health, he said the rheumatic trouble had entirely disappeared for which he was truly thankful."[38]

As had been the case with the couple's engagement, the press ignored the obvious. No eyebrows were raised when Dr. Bryant, the couple's family physician, disembarked with the president and stayed as a guest at Gray Gables for ten days. In an era when pregnancy was not mentioned in news reports, Dr. Bryant's daily presence in the Cleveland household would have been dismissed by newshounds as being necessitated by Mrs. Cleveland's now noticeable condition.

Grover Cleveland was not an especially compliant patient. Frances wrote to her friend, Mrs. Joseph Jefferson, "He is hard at work on his letters. It is so dreadfully hard to do anything with him. This morning when no one noticed he got a peach and ate it. Wouldn't you think a *child* would have more sense after the narrow escape he had?"[39]

Not all of Cleveland's close associates were in on the secret. Frances wrote to the Massachusetts governor, William E. Russell,

> As the housekeeper, I think it is my privilege to thank you for the delicious salmon which came to us several days ago. . . .
>
> The President has not been writing at all since he came up for his much-needed rest, or he would have taken the matter into his own hands and told you of the pleasure you have given us—long before now.
>
> He came here completely worn out, and with an unusually bad attack of rheumatism besides. We have made him give [himself] up entirely to resting—and he is already another man. If the country hadn't been so inconsiderate as to get up this financial trouble, which necessitated the early session of Congress, and he could get another month here away from worry, I think he would be thoroughly rested.[40]

Emma was careful in her letters to Frances about any references she made to the president's health. "We are so glad to hear the President is so much better and hope he will go back to feeling quite well," wrote Mrs. Perrine in one of them. "I think you have been very industrious and accomplished a great deal. . . . You must dread having the President go back without you, but you ought to stay on as long as it will be safe for you."[41]

Not even Richard Olney, Cleveland's attorney general, was privy to the severity of the president's condition. In an undated manuscript, presumed to have been written for Cleveland's first authorized biographer, Robert McElroy, Olney recounted his memories of those July weeks. Given the nature of the nation's economic crisis, Olney's role in helping Cleveland prepare the message to Congress at its special session was essential. However, even though Olney was expected to help deliver a solution to the nation's economic problems, he was denied access to Cleveland for two weeks. He later wrote,

> After he [Cleveland] had left [Washington], it transpired that one purpose of Mr. Cleveland's trip on the Oneida was that he might submit to a serious operation. Although the greatest efforts were made to keep the matter secret, rumors that such was the case got about and were published in the newspapers. They seemed to be verified by the fact that the yacht anchored near New York and remained stationary for a considerable period without proceeding directly to her destination. After some days, however, the yacht reached Buzzard's Bay and Mr. Cleveland was landed at Gray Gables. After an interval of a fortnight, more or less, during which I had made frequent attempts to see Mr. Cleveland, I succeeded in having an interview. He had changed a good deal in appearance, had lost a good deal of flesh, and his mouth was so stuffed with antiseptic wads that he could hardly articulate. The first utterance that I understood was something like this—"My God, Olney, they nearly killed me." He did not talk much, was very much depressed, and at the same time acted, and I believe felt, as if he did not expect to recover. Mrs. Cleveland, however, had no feeling of that sort. She was sure that he was out of danger.[42]

Dr. Bryant departed on July 30. To the public, the Clevelands maintained a very normal schedule. Cleveland fished in the morning. In the afternoon one of his clerks came to Gray Gables to take down correspondence. The president and Frances drove him to the train station, and then traveled together to see the Joseph Jeffersons.

The next few days were spent with as much of an air of normalcy as is possible when one is the president of the United States, has survived a life-threatening operation, is preparing to establish a financial policy to protect a nation from economic ruin, and has a wife who is eight months pregnant.

Frances invited the Gilders to join her at Buzzards Bay in anticipation of Cleveland's upcoming return to Washington to address Congress. A week before his scheduled departure, she wrote:

Dear H & R—

    . . . But I can't resist the temptation to beg you both to come to me the 7th for a few days. G.C. will be meeting in Washington—and Ruth and I shall be alone. I expect Mr. and Mrs. Freeman to spend that Sunday—and by Monday afternoon they will be gone—and I will make you *real comfortable*—and enjoy you so much. Of course you must not let the Cape skip a summer on seeing you—"The Cape" stands for those who love you so dearly in this house. And you can drive to Marion and to the Jeffersons for a short time. And this will be my only available time because some "Laws" [?] are coming later and we haven't so much room this year. *Please* say you will both come.

She added a quick note about Cleveland's recovery: "The President is getting rested slowly—just now the message is retarding his progress somewhat. He was worn out."[43]

Cleveland left Gray Gables for Washington to address Congress on August 5. The special session convened two days later, on August 7. When Cleveland returned to Buzzards Bay on August 12 after addressing Congress, Dr. Bryant once again accompanied him. The couple resumed their routine activities, with the president fishing daily and Frances driving into town to get the mail. Her obvious condition gave the press something to focus on in reporting about the Clevelands. "She is looking splendidly [*sic*] and appears in her usual excellent health," wrote the reporter for the *Washington Post*.[44]

The couple closed the summerhouse at the end of August, boarding E. C. Benedict's yacht on August 30 for the trip back to Washington. That same day, E. J. Edwards, a reporter for the *Philadelphia Public Ledger*, broke the story of Cleveland's surgery. Dr. Hasbrouck, who had assisted with the extractions, was said to have been the source. Edwards's editor vehemently denied the story the very next day. Not until Dr. Keen's article was published in the *Saturday Evening Post*, in 1917, was there official confirmation of what had taken place aboard the *Oneida* in early July.[45]

On Saturday, September 9, the Marine Band's weekly concert on the White House grounds was canceled. The gates to the Executive Mansion were closed.

Frances gave birth to her second child, another girl, who was named Esther. She was the first (and remains the only) presidential child ever to be born in the White House.[46]

Frances received warm and caring correspondence from many well-wishers. Kate Douglas Wiggins, with whom Frances had shared duties in the New York Kindergarten Association, wrote:

> Dear Mrs. Cleveland:
>
> If you are the first Vice President of the New York Kindergarten Ass'n, and I am the third, what relation is the new baby to me?
>
> This is not a conundrum, and therefore needs no answer. With warmest good wishes for your speedy recovery.
>
> Ever yours sincerely,
> Kate Douglas Wiggins[47]

According to her father, Esther was named for the heroine in the Bible. In a letter to Mrs. John G. Carlisle, the wife of Cleveland's secretary of the treasury, the president wrote:

> Jane is a very pretty name and there is no living person whose name I would rather our new baby should bear than yours. The responsibility of selecting her name was put upon me long before her birth and I feel that responsibility very much indeed. It may be very disappointing to those still alive whose names are passed by, but I have determined to ignore mother, grandmothers and great-grandmothers and avoid all jealousy by going back to Biblical times. I mean to call the little girl Esther. It is a favorite name with me and associated in a pleasant way with things I remember besides the hanging of Haman.
>
> You are the first one in the world, except her mother, to know the name of our second child. I hope "Jane" can wait.[48]

Cleveland's positive tone belied the newspaper reports that he was disappointed not to have a son and namesake. One said, "It is an open secret that the President is disappointed over the sex of the child, although Mrs. Cleveland expressed no surprise when told by the doctor that the child was a girl. . . . The question of naming the child, therefore, has not been discussed, although Mrs. Cleveland was long ago heard to object to the naming of a son after the president. 'There shall never be but one Grover Cleveland,' she remarked during a conversation with the wife of a member of the Cabinet."[49]

In mid-November, a small piece appeared in the *Washington Post* that was noteworthy because its occurrence was so unusual: "A pleasant domestic scene that attracted much attention was witnessed from the Treasury Department [located across from the White House] about 3 o'clock yesterday afternoon. The President and his family were in the capacious grounds south of the Executive Mansion gathering autumn leaves. . . . Mr. Cleveland every now and then picked up some of the prettiest leaves himself and presented them to his wife. When all were well supplied they returned to the house."[50]

Frances was frequently alone, as she had been during her first White House years. As Hoover wrote in his memoirs, "The family did not see much of him. He had little desire for company and he never seemed to sleep."[51]

The upcoming Christmas season with two babies in the White House offered the already intrusive public and press another opportunity to intrude on the Cleveland family's privacy. In a letter to Helena Gilder, Frances is uncharacteristically defensive about her decisions to put her children and their welfare ahead of any of her other duties.

Dec. 15, 1893
Dearest Helena,

It is such an age since I have heard from any of you and yet I know it is my own fault. I find myself very busy with my "social duties" beginning again and two babies. I give so much time to the children because I won't be cheated of their babyhood by anything—much less "not worth-while things." So I have it so that people can't see me at certain hours no matter who comes—Esther is really a lovely child—she has a great deal of beauty and I think she will be fairer than Ruth though what little hair she manages to scrape together is brown. Her lashes and eyebrows are so light and Ruth's at three months (the age at which my Esther has attained) were quite black. She is the best baby I ever *imagined.* We have been holding our breath over this these months time—because I am told their dispositions sometimes change at that age. And Ruth grows so! You know how they grow—but to me it is wonderful.[52]

In a clever ruse to avoid public attention, Frances arranged for a close friend to take Ruth to the photographer's studio. "Mrs. Cleveland one fine day last week, wishing to have her little daughter Ruth properly photographed and realizing that to take her to the establishment herself or intrust her to the nurse for that purpose with instructions to have the negatives forwarded to the White House for inspection would result in the very thing she has been so anxious to avoid—that is, to have the country flooded with pictures of the child."

The photographer sent the negatives to Frances's unnamed friend, at the friend's address, from which Frances selected the best poses. The press, after carefully scrutinizing the tens of negatives taken that day by the photographer, could not identify which pictures were those of Ruth Cleveland. "It is as the riddle of the Sphynx [*sic*]—unanswered still and likely to remain so as far as any enlightenment from the White House is concerned."[53]

Frances had good reason to protect her children from public identification. At about this same time period, information surfaced about a plot to kidnap Ruth from the White House grounds. Letters were found in Abilene, Kansas, allegedly mailed from Minneapolis, where Frances's aunt and her family lived, and Washington, DC, detailing a plan to "carry off little Ruth Cleveland and hold her until a ransom was forthcoming for her deliverance." A subsequent letter outlined the intention to deposit Ruth "in some secret place and carry off Esther, too."[54]

The public's outrageous behavior toward the two little girls resulted in Frances ordering the gates to the White House grounds closed whenever the family was in residence. "The children were the objects of insane curiosity," observed Ike Hoover in his memoir. "Once a visitor was snipping a curl from Ruth's head when stopped.

The nurses were at their wits' ends to protect their charges. Looking out one day, Mrs. Cleveland saw a nurse in tears and one baby being handed about and pawed by a crowd of fifty visitors. The mother was forced to issue an order closing the gates to the south grounds where the children took the air."[55]

Rather than recognize the Clevelands' right to privacy, the public reacted with strong indignation, and rumors circulated that the presidential couple did not want the public to see Ruth because she was defective. There could only be one answer for these "misguided women," as Colonel Crook wrote in his memoir, as to why Ruth Cleveland was no longer available for them to hold, pinch, pass around among themselves, and play with. She was a deaf mute. "If that were not enough," he added, "that her ears were malformed, and that there were other reasons for her seclusion. . . . And incredible as it may seem, such accusations were not lacking in a section of the newspaper press which was making war on the President and his political programme!"[56]

The stories followed the Clevelands beyond the White House years to their life in Princeton.

> Ruth Cleveland, my schoolmate [wrote Jean Davis in her memoir about Frances], was an intelligent and friendly child and an active playmate, climbing trees and scooting her sled down snow-covered lawns. . . . For many years (although only in places far from Princeton, where we knew better) I used to hear the gossip that Ruth had been crippled, "a result of her father's sins," or feeble-minded, or with a withered hand or some other defect. I always contradicted these reports. I remember particularly a woman I met at a summer hotel. When she learned that I lived in Princeton, she told some tale about Ruth. I denied it. She insisted: "I *know* it is true! I have the facts direct from Washington! A Senator told me, himself." "But *I* knew Ruth." "You were only a child, you wouldn't have noticed." An eleven-year-old would not have noticed whether the bright child in the same schoolroom was feeble-minded? Whether the girl who climbed trees and pulled a sled up

a slope was crippled? Thus early was I inoculated against gossip and taught never to take seriously any report "direct from Washington."[57]

The year 1893 drew to a close on a modest social note. The shining star of the 1886–87 Washington social scene was now a matron with two young daughters. Her husband had survived a life-threatening operation, and he was not in the best of health. The nation was experiencing tremendous economic upheaval and growing international turmoil. The remaining years of the Cleveland administration would prove themselves to be more demanding and less rewarding than the four years of Cleveland's first presidential tenure.

# 8

# "The best part is . . .
# the drive with G.C."

Washington's expectations of a stellar social season did not diminish as the town looked forward to 1894. "Mrs. Cleveland is a born leader, and enjoys the duties of her position," wrote the *Washington Post*. "Society therefore could not have a more brilliant outlook for the next four years."[1]

Frances, however, had other plans for her tenure in the White House. As she had written to Helena Gilder shortly after the election, Frances was determined to focus her time and attention on the needs of her children. The *Times* reported that "the first and only public reception to be held this season by Mrs. Cleveland [was held] from 3:30 until 5:30 o'clock. It will be recalled as the largest afternoon reception ever held within the walls of the White House, where crushes have been the rule rather than the exception." The estimated attendance was six thousand people.[2]

This single reception revealed a notable shift away from Frances's very active calendar during the first Cleveland administration. Then she had won the hearts of Washington society and the average working woman by holding three public receptions weekly during the social season: her Tuesday and Thursday afternoon receptions, and her Saturday afternoon reception held to accommodate the schedules of working women.

Frances now devoted her energies to her family. "The best part is always of course the time with the children and the drive with G.C.

which is still almost a daily occurrence," she wrote to Helena Gilder, "and the days are getting so beautiful now—and the trees becoming covered so rapidly with the first exquisite feathery green."[3]

Her daily drive with Cleveland was important enough that she commented on it regularly in her letters. "We spent our day much as we do every day—with a drive in the afternoon almost our only time together," Frances wrote to Helena. "The . . . President has been ailing for three days from a most prosaic and seasonable complaint but I think he is improving."[4]

Those who knew the Clevelands intimately noticed that Frances became protective of her husband. Ike Hoover wrote, "[H]er solicitude for the President was charming to behold. She would watch over him as if he were one of the children. Never would she permit herself to be placed first; always it was he. This was particularly noticeable when they would leave the house. It was always the President who must enter the carriage first, and no matter how much he protested—which he did—it was always he first and she after."[5]

Things were not going well for Cleveland's second term. "[It] was a stormy one . . . ," wrote Barbara S. Rivette, in a local history of Cleveland.

Financial panic, depression, and labor unrest started immediately after his inauguration and continued throughout the term. He maintained his earlier style of speaking out boldly, without regard for the political consequences. And he continued his habit of working intensely until two or three in the morning when necessary.

Mrs. Cleveland began to worry about her husband's safety, and it was arranged to increase the security staff from four to twenty-seven. Two detectives from the Washington police went out with him on his drives, following in a second buggy.[6]

Frances's frequent pregnancies during the second administration were another reason for the White House's scaled-back social life. She hinted at her third pregnancy in a letter to Helena in early November:

> Dearest Helena,
>
> How I wish I could but it is not possible—the day tomorrow at Philadelphia is more than I can look forward to with solid delight. The truth is I am not very well

prepared to do anything but mope for the next two or three weeks—and you may suspect whatever you choose as a cause—and if you guess right I shall not have told anything. I am miserable and trying to appear perfectly well—which is the next worse thing to being poor and trying to appear rich. It will soon be all right but just now everything is an effort. So you will forgive me for not even wanting to come, won't you Helena dear?[7]

A week later, Frances was more explicit about her condition, and wrote that she looked forward to a legitimate reason to step back from many of her social duties. "I rather like having the children near together," she acknowledged to Helena, "—and I dare say 'this' [her pregnancy] will keep me out of a lot of hard work this winter so I am far from broken hearted—and I feel that it is only fair to their father to have them as young as he can. Only the first few weeks wear on me at all and they are now so near over."[8]

Although Frances reduced the number of White House events, she was far more active in charity work than she had been in the first administration. At the end of 1893, at a request from Richard Watson Gilder, she had resigned from her position as vice president of the New York Kindergarten Association. With her absence from New York, and the fund-raising needs of the association, she was no longer as effective in her role as vice president as she had been while residing in the city.

However, Frances continued actively to promote the development of kindergartens in Washington. She adopted the Columbus Kindergarten as a favored charity, and attended fund-raisers for that school.[9] She lent her support to events of the Pensoara Free Kindergarten.[10]

Just before Ruth Cleveland's fifth birthday, in October 1896, Frances secured the services of Mary Bannister Willard, the sister of her close friend Katherine Willard and a trained kindergarten teacher. Mary Willard taught kindergarten in the White House, and among her students were Ruth Cleveland, Margaret Bissell, and several other children of the administration's officials. Unlike private tutoring, the kindergarten was the first formalized schooling of its kind in the White House. The move was also significant, because nearly all of the initial free kindergartens that had been established nationwide, including those supported by Frances, had been designed to teach young children—and, by extension, their mothers—how to behave properly in American society. With this move, Frances quietly introduced the concept that the young benefited from formal early education, regardless of their economic status.[11]

In another public show of support for public education for all economic levels, Frances hosted a reception for the attendees of the First Congress of Mothers in February 1897, just a few short weeks before the Clevelands moved out of the White House at the end of their term. The congress, which eventually became the national Parent-Teacher Association, was founded on the premise that all women, but especially mothers, held the key to the success of children. Consequently, mothers should have a good understanding of what was needed to help their children be successful adults. Attendance at the congress and the subsequent White House reception was estimated at eighteen hundred people.

The message of one of the congress's speakers, Mrs. Mary Lowe Dickinson of New York, president of the National Council of Women, reflected Frances's values and motivations behind much of the charity work she undertook throughout her life.

> As mothers especially [observed Mrs. Dickinson], who would fain see better things in the future that is to be the inheritance of our children we rejoice in the fact that there never before was a time when at the heart of every movement, large or small, lay such consideration for the welfare of human beings as today. Never before was so much strength, time, and money expended for the education of the illiterate. Never before were there such wise and wonderful projects for preventing pauperism and disease. Never before was the spirit of Christianity so active in human affairs. Never was religion so patient with ignorance, so pitiful to suffering, so ready to shake off the shackles put upon it by bigotry and to represent by its loving activity the power of the love of Christ.[12]

Frances's attitudes were neatly summed up by a society writer for the *Atlanta*. "Mrs. Cleveland interests herself comparatively little in private charities. She rarely sees those who apply for aid, and she never gives alms from the door. She believes in organized charity. So, aside from paying her servants and her seamstress very big wages, and paying full price for everything she buys, she does little individual giving. But to organized work, whether it be for working girls' clubs, news boys' lodging houses or church fairs, her purse strings are ever untied."[13]

The "servant issue," as it was known in Frances's day, resulted from the growing demand of educated and affluent women to be free of the daily drudgery of household and child care. Frances promoted free kindergartens as a safe, educational environment for the children of the immigrant women that she and her contemporaries employed. And, conversely, Frances employed domestic help, including nurses and kindergarten teachers, so that she could be free to pursue her own charitable and cultural interests.

Frances was known for being a fair and sympathetic employer. Finding and keeping good servant help was a struggle for much of the upper class. Frances had the added burden of finding help to maintain the White House and the Clevelands' home at Woodley, and nurses to care for their children.

> She was no more successful a hostess than wife, mother and mistress of the household [Ike Hoover wrote in his memoir]. She made each of us feel that she was personally interested, remembered us at Christmas and on our birthdays, when she could learn them, and was, all in all, the definition of a lady. She was worshipped by the staff as no other since has been. I can't describe her better than by telling of the time when she returned home unlooked for and found the fireman, a German and a musician, banging away at the piano in the library while several of the girl help danced. Any of them would have accepted it as cause for instant discharge, but Mrs. Cleveland insisted that they go on, actually put them at ease, sat down comfortably on a sofa, looked on and applauded, nor ever reproached them later.[14]

"Mrs. Cleveland is always particularly courteous, and speaks as if she were talking to people for whom she has high respect and even regard," wrote the *New York Times* about her household management style.[15] It continued,

> Another idea which Mrs. Cleveland sees carried out in the management of her servants is to provide them with the means of amusement. They cannot only have nights "out," but nights "in." And they are encouraged to enjoy themselves like privileged members of society in the Clevelands' home. . . . There are no restrictions as long as the household duties are faithfully performed. Neither are any inquiries made upon religious topics. But all are required to attend some church. With such rational ways of dealing with the "servant-girl question," it is no wonder that Mrs. Cleveland does not find it a perplexing one.[16]

German and music were two of Frances's strongest interests during these years. She hired a German nurse for Ruth, in part so that her daughter could be taught the language, and had Esther learning to speak it before she had turned two years old. Her intense learning, and the education she gave her children in German language and culture, would be upended less than twenty years later with the start of World War I.

Frances's philanthropic activities continued to mask her keen political insights, as demonstrated in a letter she wrote to Helena when Secretary Olney was moved to the head of the State Department.

> Dearest Helena,
>
> I am wondering what R. thinks of the new Cabinet appointments. I am so pleased myself and so glad G.C. hasn't the anxiety of working a new man into so important a place as the State Department. He and Mr. Olney know each other so well and they work together so well and Mr. Olney has for a long time been so much in their "foreign counsels" or councils—all of which I feel I must have written to you and yet have I written since the appointments.
>
> I wish I could send you something beside dull letters—but you must do the brilliant writing from your

side. I quite agree with your theory that the periods of a woman's life are rather brain stratifying and there aren't any events of great interest to relate to make up for my own deficiency.[17]

Frances was in her last few weeks of pregnancy when she wrote this letter. Her comment to Helena about writing "dull letters" reveals a rare insight into Frances's character: the frustration that she experienced between fulfilling the role of a wife and mother, and the strong need that she had for intellectual stimulation and activity. Frances looked for ways to find success and fulfillment within the constraints of her world.

Her marriage to Cleveland, who was a full generation older than she, led her to try to straddle the line dividing two groups. On the one side of the line were the women of her husband's generation who, regardless of intellect, put all of their energies into child rearing and homemaking. On the other side were the college-educated women of her own generation, who had a desire for travel and an interest in a world beyond the home.

Marion Cleveland was born July 7, 1895, at the Clevelands' home at Buzzards Bay. The press, with what appears to be a touch of derision, reported that the presidential couple was now the parents of three daughters. "Although the country at large insist that no more girls are wanted," Emma Folsom Perrine wrote to Helena Gilder, "the President and Mrs. Cleveland seem perfectly content and I am sure that is all that is necessary. The little girls are too delighted with their new sister for words. Their faces beam all over when she is mentioned but of course you know all about that."[18]

Marion was named for the summer community that had become the Clevelands' first true home. Frances wrote the Gilders,

Dearest Helena and R.

I am only to write a line, but I want to ask you how you feel about our calling the new baby Marion.

I have always loved the name, but I never dreamed of calling this little girl by it until she was two or three days old (I always said she w'd be a girl). Then it suddenly came to me that she must be Marion. I associate the name so much with you two. We say she is named for nothing and nobody but I think of you both quietly to myself *always* with her name. She is a dear little dark Ruth kind of baby. She gained her pound (lacking two ounces) in her 2d week. And she is so good. I am gaining splendidly. Have been out of doors today and walked from my room to the dining room to see my birthday table. I could not see it yesterday.[19]

As the second Cleveland administration drew to a close, the question for the couple was where to move. They had entered the White House as a family of three, two adults and a baby, and during their four-year tenure they had grown to a household of five. When they exited the White House in March 1897, Frances was expecting their fourth child. New York City, which had appeal in the early years of their marriage as a place of employment for Cleveland and as a social and cultural community for Frances, was not where the couple wanted to raise their growing family.

Financially, the couple was comfortable enough. Although Frances spent heavily on clothing and carriages, and Cleveland typically bought her diamonds for her birthdays, their anniversaries, and Christmas, Cleveland did not have to have a steady income. His natural conservatism had proven itself with the sound investments he had made over the years, and Frances earned an income from property she had inherited through her father's family. Cleveland owned at least one hunting lodge in the Carolinas, and the couple owned property in Lakewood, New Jersey, and their summer home at Buzzards Bay.

According to Cleveland's biographer, Allan Nevins, the couple came up with the idea of Princeton during a conversation about their future beyond the White House. In late 1896, Cleveland had visited the community, and in spite of the fact that he was the father of three girls, was greeted with a sign, "Grover, send your boys to Princeton." Frances, meanwhile, had gone to Westchester, outside of New York City, to look at houses.

She came down to breakfast one morning, and told her husband, "I have had an inspiration about our future home." "So have I," said Cleveland. Simultaneously, they asked each other. "What is it?" and simultaneously each replied, "Princeton!"[20]

Cleveland wrote Andrew F. West, professor of classics at Princeton, and West encouraged the soon-to-be-former-president to consider a move. Frances located and arranged for purchase of a home, and she oversaw the move while Cleveland went hunting after the McKinley inaugural on March 4, 1897.

The departure from the White House was a bittersweet one for Frances. Cleveland disagreed with the politics of William Jennings Bryan, the nominee of his own party, and so the Clevelands encouraged the White House staff to do everything it could to ease the transition between them and the incoming "Major and Mrs. McKinley." "No President has been more jubilant over his own reelection than Cleveland was over McKinley's rather narrow victory," wrote Ike Hoover in his memoirs.[21]

"Their leaving called for more packing than usual. Their own liberality inspired liberality, and personal presents had rained in for four years, from scented toothpicks up," he noted.[22]

As Cleveland attended the inaugural ceremonies, Frances sent word that she wanted to speak to each member of the White House staff. "Many of us wept our affection for her," Hoover observed, "while she seemed, as always complete mistress of herself."[23] However, those who were the last to say their good-byes found a less composed first lady:

> The last comers . . . found her gazing out a north window at the presidential party entering the carriages below. When she turned, her eyes were wet, and in an instant she was crying as if her heart would break. When she recovered herself, she said that she would not have us think that her tears were for the presidency, but for a home she had come to as a girl and bride and now was quitting as a mature woman.
>
> Completely composed again, she left and the Cleveland years were done.[24]

Helena deKay Gilder, an accomplished artist, offered her studio in Marion, Massachusetts, as a haven for the nation's growing artistic community. Marion became a retreat for the Clevelands from the pressures of the White House.

Grover Cleveland and Richard Watson Gilder at Buzzards Bay, Massachusetts. These two unlikely companions developed a close friendship that lasted until Cleveland's death in 1908.

A photo by C. M. Bell of Frances, dated 1894, the year after she had given birth to her second child, Esther. Few photos exist of her during her childbearing years, when her weight fluctuated.

Frances's spaniel, Kay. Frances loved animals, especially dogs, and typically owned at least two or three at a time. She once wrote to Helena Gilder that Kay was jealous of Frances even "kissing the President."

Frances's mother, Emma Folsom Perrine, and the Clevelands' two older daughters, Ruth and Esther. Following the death of her second husband, Henry Perrine, Emma became a permanent member of Frances's household.

Frances with Ruth.

Henry Perrine, Emma Folsom's second husband. Emma remarried in 1889 and lived in Buffalo until Perrine's death in 1901.

Marion Cleveland at her debut. Marion's first marriage, to Stanley Dell, ended in divorce. A year later, she married John Harlan Amen, a roommate of her brother Richard. Amen was a prosecutor during the Nazi war crime trials following the end of World War II. Marion, like her mother, devoted her energies to women's organizations, and became the coordinator of volunteers for the Girl Scouts.

Richard Falley Cleveland, the older of the Clevelands' sons, became an attorney and moved to Baltimore, Maryland, the home of his paternal grandmother. Cleveland represented Whittaker Chambers, a confessed spy who was the government's key witness in the Alger Hiss trial. Frances would sit in the visitors' section of the courtroom and knit while her son argued cases. She died in Richard's home the day before his fiftieth birthday.

Esther Cleveland at her debut. Esther served as a volunteer during World War I, and married W. S. B. Bosanquet, a British soldier. She stayed in England until her husband's death, in 1960, when she returned to the United States.

Francis Grover Cleveland, the youngest of the five Cleveland children, was not quite five years old when his father died. He inherited his mother's love of theater and his father's skills as a raconteur, and made a successful career as an actor and owner of the Barnstormers, a summer theater located near Tamworth, New Hampshire. Frances would sell tickets and her second husband, Thomas Preston, would serve as usher during the theater's performances.

Gray Gables, the Clevelands' home at Buzzards Bay, Massachusetts, was the one place where the family could retreat from the pressures of public life. They purchased the property after spending several summers visiting with the Gilders, whose place at Marion was nearby. The death in 1904 of their eldest child, Ruth, from diphtheria ended their summers here. The place held too many painful memories for the family.

In 1904, the Clevelands purchased Intermont, in Tamworth, New Hampshire. They learned of the community from their new friends, John and Martha Finley, who replaced the Gilders as close confidantes. Frances maintained her friendship with the couple after Cleveland's death in 1908, and the close relationship continued after Frances's marriage to Thomas J. Preston, Jr., in 1913. The Finleys' son delivered the eulogy at Frances's funeral.

Frances with Ruth and Esther at Gray Gables. The other woman in the photograph is unidentified, but is likely the children's nurse.

# *9*

# "Mr. Cleveland died
# at nine this morning"

Frances oversaw the family's move into its new Princeton home, while Cleveland took his annual birthday hunting trip in the Carolinas. The Georgian-style house, known as "Westland" for Andrew West, the president of Princeton University, was located on Bayard Lane, at the edge of town. It gave the Clevelands privacy, room for the children to run, and an opportunity for the couple to become involved in the activities of the university. "It was surrounded by pleasant lawns," Jean Davis, a playmate of the Cleveland children, wrote in her memoir. "What impressed me about it were the ample built-in wardrobes"; her own home, she said, "provided inadequate closet space."[1]

Within a few weeks of the move, Frances was invited to a round of teas to introduce her to Princeton society. She quickly began working locally on behalf of improving the educational and social opportunities for women. "Mrs. Cleveland was one of the very few college graduates among the ladies of the area," wrote Davis.

> My mother was another, an 1884 graduate of the University of California. May Margaret Fine had recently graduated from Wellesley. Each year added a few more, and when there began to be openings for women as teachers, librarians and secretaries, my mother and Mrs. Cleveland were among the organizers of the local College Club with the two aims of providing a social life for these young women

and encouraging other girls to enter college. The founders of the Princeton College Club were active in urging the Government of New Jersey to open educational opportunities to girls equal to those available to boys at Rutgers. It was partly due to their efforts that the New Jersey College for Women was established at New Brunswick.[2]

The Clevelands immersed themselves in the academic and social life of the community. They became regulars at Princeton's football games. The couple opened their home and shared hospitality with many of Princeton's students, giving particular attention to "the boys," young men who were living far from home and whose financial resources did not allow them to travel frequently to see their families. Quietly and unobtrusively, the Clevelands generously supported Princeton students in need with various forms of scholarships and other types of financial assistance.[3]

The Cleveland's fourth child, and first son, Richard Falley Cleveland, was born at Westland on October 30, 1897. Frank wrote the Gilders on November 2,

> Dearest Helena (and R),
>     Just a line to tell you how nice I think it is to have a Richard in the family and that I find boys (or a boy) aren't so bad after all. He is *lovely*—as blue eyed as the rest and strong and sturdy every way. He landed in the world feet first which made me a good deal of trouble and much anxiety until he gave his lusty cry. But I have been perfectly well ever since and stronger, quicker than usual. . . . [G]ive my love to all.[4]

Frances enjoyed family life without the trappings of political responsibilities. "We had a happy happy Christmas—I think the happiest we have ever had. But didn't I feel 'grown up' to say the least, with my four, about the tree . . . ," she wrote to Helena on December 27, 1897.[5]

Cleveland's health continued to be an ever-present concern, and in the months immediately following his presidency, his childlike behavior frustrated the usually unruffled Frances.

[T]he President is laid low again today with his old [trouble] in the right foot after nearly a week of feeling splendidly, which had followed two weeks of big shoe [she wrote Richard Gilder in March 1898]. He is low in his mind—and cross over the gigantic pile of invitations and things which accumulate weekly on his desk and in the same breath is sure that everybody has forgotten him—[he thinks] he is no use to anybody any more. I wish so earnestly he had some absorbing interest to get his mind out of the rut of little nuisances.

I ought to have written you long ago. The truth is I am too busy for a country woman—what with a husband to amuse at billiards and cribbage—four children—calls to make. The gay social life of Princeton (really!) and the "boys"—and now in three weeks Base Ball will begin again!

Richard the Small is growing splendidly.[6]

The future president, Woodrow Wilson, was a professor of political science at Princeton when the Clevelands moved there. His daughter, Eleanor, was one of Ruth's playmates, and she recorded her experiences in the Cleveland home in her memoir. "Mrs. Cleveland, a great beauty, wore clothes that were a topic of lively discussion among the children, not only because they were smart, but because she had so many," wrote Wilson.

Wilson and her sister, Margaret, were invited to Ruth Cleveland's birthday party. "My sister sat at Mrs. Cleveland's right and the salad, elaborately arranged in three half cantaloupes, was passed to her [Margaret] first. She took one of the halves, the child next to her hesitated a moment and then did the same, and the third child took all that remained of the salad. After some delay more was produced, a different sort entirely, and placed in the exact center of a large bowl, sans decoration. Then, of course, everyone realized what had happened."[7]

Frances abandoned her Princeton decorum during the summer months at Gray Gables. Photographs taken in the late 1890s show the Clevelands at their most relaxed, with Frances's mother, Emma, in a bathing costume, Frances sunburned and dressed simply, and clothing and towels hung around the porch rail that encircled the house. One photograph captures the president and Frances standing on a dock, most likely with their friend Commodore Benedict, laughing at some shared joke. The photo is rare for the casualness it portrays.

For Frances, happiness was the opportunity to read and study. While Cleveland spent his days fishing, she spent hers reading, often in French, German, and Italian—in all of which she was fluent.

She was particular about keeping track of her books, which led to an interesting correspondence with President Theodore Roosevelt in the early summer of 1902, precipitated by "the enclosed paper in a book," a copy of a letter regarding the gift of a volume of works by Dante, that she found.

> Dear Mr. President.
>
> I found the enclosed paper in a book the other day—a volume of Dickens—and I have not been able to get it out of my head—as well as you can imagine. I knew nothing of the book's coming. I never heard of it that I can remember. I feel sure it is not among our books—and I wonder if it could be in the White House libraries. It seems a small matter with which to trouble the President—just a book—but after all a valuable edition of Dante, sent by the King of Italy to the President, isn't such a little thing—and I feel perfectly sure you will be willing to set the hunt going.
>
> Very sincerely,
> Frances F. Cleveland[8]

Two weeks later, Frances again wrote:

> Dear Mr. President.
>
> I would not trouble you again about the Dante; but I want to thank you, and to tell you that the one sent is not the right one. The book mentioned in Mr. Bayard's memorandum must have been in Italian and a recent edition with old notes which had just been discovered. The one sent me was a Cory translation with Doré illustrations, an edition I remember well in the White House library.

It is surely possible that the one I am seeking is somewhere among our books, but hardly likely as I think I know pretty well what we have.[9]

Notes scribbled at the top of the letter include the words "look carefully," and shorthand notes dictated to respond to Frances's letter. There is no record that the correct Dante was ever located.

On May 30, 1901, Frances's stepfather, Henry Perrine, died. He and Emma had been married for twelve years, and the two had lived in Buffalo during that time. Perrine's children from his first marriage received the proceeds from his estate, including his home, and Emma was once again a permanent resident of the Cleveland household.[10]

In her annual Christmas letter to her friend, Martha Waller Johnson, Frances wrote: "With love to all (You know my mother is with us all the time now.) from all of us."[11]

More was changing than simply the addition of Frances's mother to the Clevelands' daily lives. Cleveland's health, which had never been the best, began a slow, steady decline. In the same letter to Johnson, Frances wrote: "We have all been well except Mr. Cleveland—his illness has kept him housed six weeks already, but he is beginning to come downstairs. The pneumonia made him very little trouble, taking itself off in a very respectable and decent manner, but gout set in. That has kept him prisoner ever since."[12]

With her usual equanimity, Frances wrote to Martha Waller Johnson in early March 1903, "We are all well, and I hope your cold has left you entirely. I am planning for a new little Cleveland in July, so while I am, as I say, well, I am not 'up to' everything. Don't speak of it unless you are asked, please. You understand how I feel about it!"[13]

Francis Grover, the Clevelands' youngest child, was born on July 18, 1903, and his birth helped Frances cope with her profound grief when her eldest daughter, Ruth, died seven months later from diphtheria, on January 7, 1904.

What started in Ruth as a simple sore throat quickly gave way to a disease that also claimed others in the community, and for which there was no cure. Frances's letter to Helena and Richard Gilder, written five days later, was a poignant testimony to Frances's lifetime discipline of putting others first.

Jan. 12, 1904
Dearest H & R,

I want you to know that we are all well—Dr. Bryant had cultures taken of all the throats in the house—& no germs were found. And I want you to know how much we are leaning on your love & how much strength it gives. If I keep looking back & up I see so much beauty & so much to be thankful for—& try not to look ahead nor to think of the loneliness without that beautiful cheerful life beside me. She was not a child—never a mother had more to be thankful for.

Ruth was quite worried that Rosamond did not get her little Christmas pencil, which was in the package addressed to Francesca—she asked us several times if I thought she didn't because Francesca said "we were much obliged for the frame." She bought and planned all her little gifts herself this year & had such a happy Christmas. The illness began Saturday & I knew she was very ill—though sure when the culture was taken there was no real fear of diphtheria. I was with her most of the time—& did not leave her from [early] morning when the results came—until after six when the nurse came—the same one Esther had & loved so much. The anti-toxin was given about 11 a[.]m. The earliest moment it could be obtained—& when I left her she was perfectly better & contented & she slept until nearly two when they called to us as her heart action was very weak. The nurse would not let me go to her—although it nearly broke her heart but Ruth did not know & she did not suffer.

I wrote so far Saturday & could not finish. Thanks for your dear words & R's lovely little poem. Today I can & do realize how much we have to be thank[ful] for—in that the others have been spared *this* attack. Everything was sad—but everything was beautiful—no *horror* of any kind.

Lovingly,
Frank
She is in her little bed [grave] by Margaret Finley—I
have loved the spot ever since that dear little friend was
placed there & there is no place in Princeton that I have
known better in the last two years.[14]


John and Martha Finley had moved to Princeton in 1900. Finley,
like Gilder, had a background in magazine publishing; he had been
the editor of *Harper's Weekly*. Upon his arrival at the university, Finley assumed the chairmanship of the Political Science Department at
Princeton, and the couples became good friends. Frances and Martha
shared a birthday, and the loss of a daughter to each drew the families
even closer together.

A week after Ruth's death, Martha wrote to Helena Gilder:

My dear Mrs. Gilder,
Mrs. Cleveland tells me that she has written to you
once, but I am sure you will want to know again how they
are. I can well imagine how you have sympathized and
mourned with them, and how full of anxious thoughts your
heart and Mr. Gilder's have been. Mrs. Cleveland's faith
and courage are beautiful beyond expression. Wonderful
as she is under all the circumstances she has ever known,
she is more wonderful now in her sorrow. You will see her
face has a new beauty in it, and she keeps it bright for
her husband and children.[15]


Ruth's death altered the Clevelands' relationship with the Gilders.
The Clevelands abandoned their home at Buzzards Bay. Memories
of Ruth at their Gray Gables home were too strong. They spent the
summer of 1904 with the Finleys, and purchased a home nearby in
Tamworth, New Hampshire, which they named "Intermont."

Cleveland's health continued to deteriorate following Ruth's
death.

In an interview conducted with Francis Grover Cleveland in
1984, the youngest of the Cleveland children shared his memories

of his father during one of the last family photograph sessions taken before Cleveland died:

> There's a famous photo of me and my father sitting on the porch of our home in Princeton. "I'm holding a teddy bear. I remember I raised a stink because I didn't want my picture taken, and he pacified me with the teddy bear.
>
> One night I went to see him before bed. I remember his mustache and cigar. His nose was running. He was very ill. Strangely enough, I can't remember anything else. It's terrible.[16]

In her annual Christmas note to Martha Johnson at the end of 1907, Frances wrote:

> I wish you could see how full my days are and how difficult it is for me to get done what I do. You would forgive me. I wish, too, you could have seen Mr. Cleveland with the beaten biscuit [a gift from the Johnsons]! He took them to NY in his pocket twice, and had his entire lunch off them!
>
> I ought to have borne it in mind that he could not write you himself. He is really better, but not strong yet, and of course he has to be very careful.[17]

In early March, the following year, Frances wrote again to Martha:

> Your letter of a few weeks ago has been lying on my desk to be answered, but I have had so much writing to do in Mr. Cleveland's illness that some things I have meant to do, I have not done. . . .
>
> Mr. Cleveland is getting on very satisfactorily, considering he must be sick at all!—He had several weeks ago two attacks near together of his old digestive trouble, and though they yielded soon to treatment he was left in a weakened condition—and it will probably be some time before he regains his usual strength. Our experience of

last summer teaches us that it is likely to be slow.—The newspapers are perfectly abominable. I give out statements to the Associated Press, telling just how he is—but they aren't content with the truth and want a sensation. It's very trying to our friends.[18]

Frances continued to treat Cleveland's illness as nothing out of the ordinary. Whether her perceived calmness in her correspondence was the result of her years of self-discipline in hiding her true feelings or a genuine belief that Cleveland was not dying is hard to determine. In early April she wrote to Helena:

Dearest Helena,
"My Man" had a very hard time last week. Poor Dear, he does have to suffer so much pain & distress in this miserable trouble of his! But he has been gaining finally & has been comfortable & contented. We have planned to go home today or tomorrow [from Lakewood, NJ] but he decided Wednesday we might as well wait a few days longer. He had a pretty bad night last night. I tell you Helena "Bowels" are awful things & he suffered great pain. But at last he is comfortable and asleep. This seems to be some temporary affair of indigestion & I hope it will be all right when he wakes up. He isn't very strong & tires easily but that is very natural after such an attack as he had last week.[19]

A few weeks later, Frances wrote to Helena:

I am so sorry—but my husband isn't strong enough to see any one & won't be for several days & I am going back to Princeton tomorrow for Sunday, as Esther is going to join the church. Mr. Cleveland has been sick again. We have tried to keep it as quiet as possible as it does so alarm his sisters when they get the reports. I came over Tuesday a.m.—having been here Monday & left him while not really well. I supposed [him] better than he had been. They called me Tuesday early. That day & Wednesday were anxious ones. The trouble would not yield, but finally late that night he became better—& now it is only to regain strength & he must go very slow.[20]

When it was clear that Cleveland's health was not improving, the couple returned to their home in Princeton. Frances was with her husband when he died, on June 24, 1908. Her telegram to Richard Watson Gilder read: "Mr. Cleveland died at nine this morning. Mrs. Cleveland"[21]

Cleveland had been a presence in Frances's life since her birth in 1864. From the time that he purchased her first baby carriage, through his guiding hand in her education and as a spouse, the father of her children and provider during twenty-two years of marriage, Grover Cleveland had been vital to her world. Now Frances was a widow and the sole parent of four children who ranged in age from almost five to almost fifteen.

Richard Watson Gilder was at his New York home when his office called to tell him that word was out on Wall Street that Cleveland was dead. Frances telegrammed Gilder at both his home and his office, but the phone call reached him first. He went immediately to Princeton, and Frances asked him to help her plan the funeral.[22]

As Cleveland had not died in office, Frances decided that he would prefer not to have a state funeral. The pallbearers were those who had been his closest friends in his later years, and she placed "by the head the closest friends, those that she knew had the most love for him, and that he himself cared most for, and she asked us to carry him—not have paid carriers, and this we were so glad to do."[23]

Frances had lost none of her antipathy for the press in the years since she had left the White House, and members of the nation's five major newspapers appealed to Gilder to assist them in obtaining information for a "great historical event . . . about which they were greatly lacking details."[24] Gilder, while expressing the understanding typical of a journalist, also understood and respected Frances's wishes.

Emma Perrine was in Tamworth with the children when Cleveland died, and Richard and Esther, as the eldest son and daughter, were sent back to Princeton to attend the funeral. The ceremony took place in the reception room of Westland, with the overflow crowd gathering in the home's library. President and Mrs. Theodore Roosevelt attended, along with members of Cleveland's cabinet and other high public officials. *Harper's Weekly* reported, "There were present the members of the family and those officials of the government whose significance [*sic*] of their desire to attend, Mrs. Cleveland had acceded to notwithstanding her wish, amounting almost to an uncompromising determination, to keep the funeral a purely private family function." Failing in that, the family kept Cleveland's body upstairs, away from the crowds, permitting only immediate relatives to view it before the closed coffin was brought downstairs for the funeral. Cleveland was buried next to his daughter, Ruth, in the Princeton cemetery.[25]

Coverage of Cleveland's death was not limited to a retrospective of his life or the details of his funeral. Newspapers published information about the supposed value of his estate. The day after Cleveland's death the *New York Times* reported, "Contrary to the general belief, Mr. Cleveland was a poor man."[26]

While Cleveland never attained the wealth of some of his closest business and political associates, such as Richard Olney, Richard Watson Gilder, Francis Lynde Stetson, or J. P. Morgan, Cleveland was far from impoverished.

In addition to his Princeton and Tamworth properties, there was his home at Buzzards Bay, which Cleveland sold, and Frances sold the cottage at Lakewood the following year. Frances also owned property in Nebraska, on which she made improvements and paid the taxes.[27] Cleveland's will, according to one news report, left his "dear wife, Frances," as the executor of his estate, and a trust of $10,000 each for the education of their children.

Apart from the Clevelands' real estate holdings, Cleveland owned significant shares of stock. A report of his safe deposit box holdings as of February 14, 1905, showed that he owned one hundred shares each of preferred stock in the Southern Railway Company, twenty-five shares in the New York Security and Trust Company, and ten bonds, valued at $1,000 each, in the Marquette, Houghton, and Ontonagan Railroad. The same report shows that Frances held, in trust for the children, twelve bonds in the Northern Pacific Railroad and one hundred shares of preferred stock in the United States Rubber Company.[28]

Frances's cash position was apparently strong enough to gain the attention of Andrew Carnegie, who encouraged her to deposit her funds in his private bank in exchange for earning 6 percent interest. Frances had befriended the Carnegies through her social activities in New York, and had secured a donation from Andrew Carnegie for the erection of a library on the Wells campus that bore her name.

Frank Hastings, who served as a coexecutor with Frances, questioned Carnegie's actions. Carnegie, in a telegram to Hastings, sent from Carnegie's home at Skibo Castle, Dornoch, Sutherland, in Scotland, and dated September 29, 1908, wrote reassuringly:

> What I volunteered to do for Mrs. Cleveland is what I have done for many of my friends. I take all their money and it is entered as a debt on my Estate, bearing 6% interest, payable semi-annually, the principal subject to withdrawal at any time. I do not trouble my friends, who in many cases are women, and in others, artists, ministers and professional men, with the responsibilities of investing. They have my Estate for their debt. Of course a receipt is sent to each one and the money is free for their use at any time.
>
> During the recent panic in our Country, I received letters from more than one of my friends thanking me that they could rest soundly at night, having no fear for their little patrimony.
>
> My receipt for the debt will be good. I have no debts but of one kind, those of my friends who have made me their banker.
>
> I shall be glad to see you on my return to New York and arrange everything to your own satisfaction. There is no name on my list for whom I should more gladly stand as Trustee than dear Mrs. Cleveland.[29]

The disposition of her funds was not the only burden that Frances encountered upon Cleveland's death. A day before Carnegie sent his telegram to Hastings, she had written Carnegie regarding the publication in the *New York Times,* on August 30, 1908, of an article that was supposedly written by Cleveland prior to his death.[30] The writer Broughton Brandenburg had contacted her in early August, claiming that he had the first of a series of articles for which he had contracted with Cleveland. Brandenburg told Frances that the contract agreement between him and Cleveland was for $2,000, but that he (Brandenburg) was willing to settle with the estate for less, since the entire series could no longer be written.[31]

Frances initially believed the information to be correct, and she instructed Hastings to negotiate with Brandenburg. According to her letter to Carnegie, "My suspicions were aroused [a few days later] by an enquiry from the New York Herald about an interview which had been offered them purporting to be by Mr. Cleveland and supporting Mr. Taft—and criticising the Southern people—also by notice received from a friend in Magazine circles that a man named Brandenburg—a rather shady character in those circles, was trying to dispose of an article purported to be by Mr. Cleveland. It was then that I telegraphed the Times and also Mr. Hastings, urging him to try and stop the publication."[32]

After some initial concern on Hastings' part regarding the genuineness of Cleveland's signature on a contract produced by Brandenburg, it soon became clear from the method of work described by Brandenburg and the writing style that the contract was not genuine. Hastings attempted to convince the *Times* not to print the article, but he was not successful.[33]

Frances decided to prosecute, with help from Hastings, Gilder, and her longtime friend and family physician, Dr. Joseph Bryant. The trial gained national attention. Brandenburg was charged with grand larceny, and he forfeited his bond when he failed to appear in court for a hearing on February 1, 1909. A warrant was issued for his arrest.[34]

When the hearing was finally held, in mid-June, Frances testified against Brandenburg. Her presence in the courtroom commanded instant respect, the court officials bowing when she entered. Her answers were straightforward and very clear, as she asserted that she had not talked with the defendant and that she had made a strong effort to prevent publication of the article.[35]

Brandenburg was convicted of larceny, in no small degree due, most likely, to Frances's involvement and testimony in the case.

During the time that she was following the trial, Frances began organizing a Cleveland memorial service. Cleveland's former law partner,

Francis Lynde Stetson, served as the Memorial Committee chair, and committee members included the familiar names of Richard Watson Gilder, Dr. Joseph Bryant, Andrew Carnegie, and John H. Finley.[36]

The afternoon program, held on the seventy-second anniversary of Cleveland's birth, March 18, 1909, took place at Carnegie Hall and was attended by President William Howard Taft, who spoke. Frances attended with Marion and Richard, and she was surrounded by Cleveland's sisters, nephews, and many of her closest friends from the presidential and postpresidential years.[37]

Gilder read a poem that he had written for the occasion, and Frances wrote him the following week:

> I want to write a word to tell you how beautiful the poem was. Even in that big hall, I missed no word—& you must know as I closed my eyes my mind went back to the first reading in Helena's garden. It seems absurd for me to thank you for it—but I must tell you how grateful I am—that such a friendship & *knowing* made possible the writing. I am sure it is a joy to you to do it & for that I am grateful too. It was all so gratifying—It will be a beautiful memory & ever increasingly so. I am only sorry Esther missed it.[38]

Esther missed the ceremony because she had set sail in early March for Europe with her grandmother.[39]

The plan was for Frances herself to follow with the rest of her children, once the one-year anniversary of Cleveland's death, and the Brandenburg trial, had passed.

In early September, she wrote to Martha Waller Johnson:

> We are sailing Sept 25 from Hoboken—on the Berlin of the North German . . . Line—for Genoa—whence we go to Lausanne direct and the children will be there in school. My mother, the four children, my husband's niece Mary Hastings of Hartford, our governess and my maid make the party of nine! We shall be most of the time at Lausanne—making trips of course but the girls and Richard will be there at school. . . .

We are in the dismal days one always has before sailing—feeling that we shall never see home or friends again, and wondering why we were such fools as to decide to go. Only that we'll . . . trust we shall have profit and pleasure.[40]

It was the first time Frances had been to Europe since her prenuptial trip in 1886, but it would the first of many, marking the beginning of a new life as a world traveler.

# 10

# "I am marrying
# Mrs. Grover Cleveland"

The Cleveland family's trip to Europe served as a tonic for Frances. She pursued her love of language study, and introduced her children to European culture. The tone of her letter to the Gilders reflected a renewed optimism and outlook.

> We are very regular [she wrote to Helena, on November 12, 1909].—[W]orking at writing or studying in the morning & going out all the afternoon—sight seeing, walking, shopping and generally getting our tea where we can hear good music.
>
> The children seem quite contented now. . . . They speak only French & Mlle. Barriere is *delightful*. Richard is beginning to be well now. He was sad at first so homesick and worried he would not be happy. . . . Mother and Mary go to Paris next week & I may follow them out. I don't want to at all. I am studying hard on Italian & I hate to break with it.[1]

Cleveland's legacy was never far from her mind, however. In the same letter, she expresses her appreciation for Richard Watson Gilder's memoir of Cleveland, *A Record of Friendship*, published in 1909: "Isn't it gratifying the way everyone loves RWG's article about

Mr. Cleveland! On every side I hear so much. I am glad for him—&
glad for *us*—and glad for my dear husband as so many who read
these papers will get the real insight into his work."[2]

Gilder's biographical sketch of Cleveland was the writer's last
major literary effort. Gilder's influence in the literary world had waned
in the last decade of the previous century, as American literature moved
away from the romantic idealism that Gilder espoused and toward a
realism that he disdained. Gilder's work was the first of several Cleveland biographies to be published following the late president's death,
and Gilder's diminished reputation limited the work's acclaim.

Like his presidential friend, Gilder had been battling illness
for several years, and he finally succumbed shortly after *A Record of
Friendship* was published. The Gilders had been with Frances during
the days immediately following Cleveland's death, but Frances could
not be present to support Helena in her loss. Frances expressed her
sorrow to Helena in a letter written on November 21:

> My precious friend,
>     What can I say! God bless you & give you the strength
> for this, but if I could only make you know that He will.
> I dared not write you yesterday when the cable came, until
> I had some confirmation. I prayed there might be some
> mistake. But dear Helena it is hard for me to be so far away.
> I know what you were to me those sad June days—can
> I ever forget! & If I were there I might do something to
> give a little warmth to your poor dear cold heart.
>     It is dreadful to know nothing but the two pathetic
> words—but I dare not think of any thing it all means
> to me in the face of all your grief. But I thank God for
> him—he has brought only blessing everywhere—& such
> blessing! And that makes it harder—until we have courage
> to think most of that.
>     There are so many things I must know—& some
> one will have told me—for who after his own love him
> more than I?
>         Your loving & sad, sad
>         Frank[3]

Frances and her family returned from Europe on May 29, 1910, and she resumed many of her responsibilities, including her involvement as a trustee of Wells College.[4]

In 1911, her twenty-four years of experience as a trustee enabled her to help guide the school through a time of crisis in its leadership.

In 1904, the Reverend Dr. George Morgan Ward had assumed the presidency of Wells. From the start of his tenure, he had health problems that affected his ability to govern the institution, and he used his health as a reason to spend winters in Florida.[5] Davis wrote in her memoir, "[I]t was said [that] he added to his income by regular preaching in that sunny state while the rest of the college waded through the snow in Aurora."[6]

According to the Wells College historian Jane Marsh Dieckmann, "Dr. Ward was adored by the students. He had, at times, charming manners and was very good looking if you happened to like the looks he had. Unfortunately he regarded Wells as a kind of stepdaughter, to be alternately petted and neglected. He would leave her under someone else's protection for the hard bitter winters you find in Aurora, while he and his wife went to Palm Beach, where he entertained people with his sermons and himself, quite forgetting his poor little frozen-up college."[7]

In March 1911, Nicholas Zabriskie, chairman of Wells's board of trustees, sent a personal letter noting the faculty's request for Morgan's return. His presence was needed to settle a father's request for reinstatement of his daughter, who had been suspended for cheating. Morgan's continued absence through March and April prompted a special faculty meeting, which took place on May 2, to discuss the issue.

The Frances F. Cleveland Library was dedicated at the 1911 commencement ceremonies, and there is evidence that the faculty's concerns were discussed with the trustees during that time. Carnegie's gift to the college was built at a cost of $58,000.[8]

On November 23, 1911, as agreed at their previous meeting, the trustees met in New York City at the home of the alumnae trustee Mary Boynton Swenson. According to the minutes, thirteen trustees were present, including the board president, Zabriskie, and five women on the board—four alumnae and the school's former lady principal, Helen Fairchild Smith. The trustees named a three-member committee to study the matter: Thomas Mott Osborne, a well-known prison reformer from Auburn; Grace Storrs Weston; and Frances.[9]

President Ward was absent again in January 1912, and he notified the faculty by letter that he had appointed the professor of art and archaeology, Thomas Jex Preston, Jr., to take charge of the college and preside at all faculty meetings in his absence. Preston, a Princeton man and a friend of Frances's, had been on the faculty less than a year.[10]

The choice of Preston was unusual because of his short tenure at Wells. Preston had graduated from the Brooklyn Polytechnic Institute in 1880, and he had been successful in his family's kerosene business, located in Newark, New Jersey. After selling his business at the age of forty, he studied art at the Sorbonne, in Paris, and enrolled at Princeton as its first adult undergraduate. He earned, in quick succession, a bachelor of literature degree (1906), a master of arts degree (1907), and a PhD (1911). During these years, he was appointed a fellow of classical studies in Rome and won a competitive scholarship awarded by the Archaeological Institute of America.[11]

Ward resigned under pressure in March 1912, and named Preston acting president, without the board's consent. Preston took it upon himself to move into apartments in the Main Building, known as the Prophet's Chamber, that were typically reserved as accommodations for special speakers. The Wells dean of students, Dr. Piutti, now forced to find other accommodations for visiting lecturers and preachers, protested the move. She also resented Preston's decision to eat at her table in the dining hall. Someone from the class of 1912 remarked that he was the only man in the room.[12]

Dean Piutti had no need to be concerned about Preston's length of stay. On October 29, 1912, John Grier Hibben, the president of Princeton, announced to the press that Frances Folsom Cleveland was engaged to marry Dr. Thomas Jex Preston.

On the same date, Preston informed Nicholas Zabriskie, who now served as the board-approved acting president of Wells, of his intention to resign from the faculty. Zabriskie replied, "I am sorry to hear that. Is it anything I can do something about?" Preston replied that he was resigning to marry, because there were no suitable accommodations for his bride.

Zabriskie offered to help find a suitable home, to which Preston answered, "No, I have looked into every possibility. There isn't anything going to be vacant except an apartment up over Hickey's store."

Zabriskie continued to make suggestions, none of which Preston found suitable. He reasserted that his decision to resign was final. As he was leaving Zabriskie's office, Preston asked: "Don't you want to know *whom* I am marrying? I am marrying Mrs. Grover Cleveland, that's whom I am marrying! I can't bring *her* to live over Hickey's store!"[13]

The *New York Times* carried the story the next day on the front page with the headline, "Mrs. Cleveland to Marry Again. Ex-President's Widow Announces Her Engagement to Prof. Thomas Jes [*sic*] Preston." Her engagement photo, the first published since Cleveland's death that did not show her wearing black, reveals a still startlingly attractive woman, who had lost none of her flair for stylish clothes. She had gained weight since Cleveland's death, and the photo suggests that she is wearing cosmetics.[14]

The *Citizen* described Preston this way:

> He's fifty and looks less than forty; he is 6 feet tall and wide shouldered; he's forceful and refined, almost too refined; he's retiring and hates publicity; he has black hair streaked with gray, and a black mustache; . . . he has a sense of humor that is sometimes grim; he's rich and teaches for love of the subject; he's a self-made man and made a good job of it; he smokes cigarettes, drives a racing car and has a touring car, smashes up every now and then; plays a good game of tennis and is fast on his feet; the girls call him "Arty" because he teaches art, and gossip says Mrs. Cleveland created the chair of art in Wells to make a place for him where she knew she could find him.[15]

A telegram to Helena to confirm the newspaper story suggests that Frances was following the same script that she and Cleveland had used regarding their engagement and upcoming nuptials.[16]

Frances wrote Helena on November 1:

You will understand when I can tell you everything—both
why I am doing it & why I could not tell you first. I am
happy with a peace that I cannot write you about. My
children and my mother are more than satisfied. I want
to see you.
    Lovingly,
    Frank[17]


As a public figure, Frances could not enjoy her engagement in
privacy. When the news was reported, Princeton's students unofficially
sanctioned the marriage, with the understanding that the Prestons
would live in Princeton.[18]

But Wells had a claim on the couple, too. The Executive Committee of the Eastern Association of Wells College issued a resolution
congratulating the couple, adding that the admiration felt for Dr.
Preston by the present body of students, as well as the affection of
all Wells girls who have known Mrs. Cleveland in regard to college
matters, gave rise to the hope that Aurora and not Princeton would
be the future home of Dr. Preston and his bride.[19]

Preston immediately discovered the reasons behind Frances's seemingly compulsive insistence on secrecy. Newspaper reporters swarmed
Aurora and took up posts around his lodging. Preston retreated to the
Prophet's Chamber, hoping to avoid contact with them. The reporters
merely changed tactics, milling about in the hallway outside his class-
room and intercepting students, who were only too willing to talk.

When Preston boarded a train—secretly, he thought—to travel
to Princeton, a reporter emerged from the baggage section and badgered Preston throughout the train ride in the hopes of gaining
information.[20]

Preston was quickly incorporated into Frances's social activities.
He was with Frances when her daughter, Esther, made her debut.
On January 11, 1913, President and Mrs. Taft held a White House
dinner in the couple's honor, and friends in both the Princeton and
Washington communities feted them, as well.

The White House dinner was considered the climax of the
couple's Washington visit. Employees who remembered her tenure took
extra pains to prepare for her visit. Her favorite flowers—jonquils and
pansies—were placed near her at the dinner-table seat. Her carriage

was sent around to the east entrance, so that she could observe the new arrangement for guests entering the house. She was shown the Blue Room, the place where she had married Grover Cleveland nearly twenty-seven years earlier. The guests for the engagement dinner were assembled there. "No eye present but was turned on her as she entered this room," noted Ike Hoover, who was still a White House employee, "and it was plainly evident that her inward feelings were profound. But being almost immediately reassured by the small company already assembled, she regained her composure and took her place at the right of the entrance as the honor guest of the occasion."[21]

There had been no announcement of a wedding date, and so the couple surprised the public by marrying at the home of John Grier Hibben, the president of Princeton University. Hibben performed the ceremony on February 10, 1913. Emma was in Bermuda. Richard was away at school. Preston's parents, sisters, and brother attended, along with a few close friends of the couple. The explanation for the hasty ceremony was a doctor's recommendation that Preston spend the winter in Florida as treatment for some undisclosed ailment.[22]

The day before, Frances wrote Helena:

> I want to tell you myself that it is to be tomorrow morning—God willing. Mr. Preston has been very ill, so much so that it seemed it would be a long time before we could be married & my mother went yesterday to Bermuda.—it seems the best thing for him to go away—& with me so we have fixed up our plans—& we shall get off to the South as soon as we can. I hate to think you will never know him before he is my husband, but I feel sure you will like him & if you only knew him as I know him! I can't say more than that your Richard would have been satisfied with him. This is not the enthusiasm of a girl—it is the settled conviction of a mature woman—whose standards of men you know.
>
> I won't see you for sometime—unless you go to Florida. Let me hope you will. I know your love & good wishes—*how* I value them!
>
> Lovingly,
> Frank[23]

Some did not welcome Frances's marriage. Jean Davis captured much of the prevailing public sentiment in her memoir:

> I remember the unpleasant shock when I read the head-lines reporting the engagement. Mrs. Cleveland, like Mrs. [Jacqueline] Kennedy after her, was a national monument and it distressed many of us to learn that the base was of clay. Besides, I knew her children, and I knew how I myself might have dreaded the arrival of a stepfather. And that it was Mr. Preston! I knew his *back* well, as I had known that of his predecessor at "Westland." Until the mid nineteen-thirties the First Presbyterian Church of Princeton was supported by pew rents. Plate collections were for missions. The Cleveland pew was third in front of ours. The broad back of the ex-President had long been familiar to me. So now his place was taken by a younger, less corpulent man, with shiny black hair, who wore a shepherd-plaid sports coat to church in an era when we were accustomed to gentlemen who dressed in Sunday morning formality.[24]

Davis's remark about Frances's "feet of clay" is a curious one. While it is certainly true that Frances, like every other human being, had her foibles, Grover Cleveland's had become forgotten. History recalled the secret romance of the couple, the exchange of letters between a young bride-to-be and her anxious, if middle-aged, groom.

Without a television news cycle and in the absence of hundreds of reporters assigned to chronicle the smallest details of family life, much of the Cleveland relationship remained private and personal—just the way the Clevelands wanted it. Letters and memoirs reveal that the Cleveland marriage, like many of the affluent marriages of the time, was a union of two people with separate interests living under a common roof. Frances never lost that sense of aloneness that was a constant presence in her marriage to Cleveland.

Cleveland was the financial provider and official head of the household. Frances managed all of the daily affairs, from overseeing the household staff—which consisted of maids, cooks, and nurses—to paying the bills and caring for their children. Cleveland took frequent hunting trips, including his annual birthday trip. When he was home at Princeton, he was typically ensconced in his study writing or working; when at Buzzards Bay and later, Tamworth, he was in a fishing boat for as many hours as he could be.

By contrast, Preston was a man who shared many of Frances's interests. The two of them traveled extensively to Europe, South America, and Asia. They shared similar interests in the arts and music. And Preston, unlike the provincial and self-taught Cleveland, was conversant in several languages, well-educated, and well-read.

He was also a gifted musician and needleworker. He played the piano beautifully, and when Frances pulled out her ever-present knitting needles, Preston picked up his crocheting. He was once quoted as saying, "[I]t was all right for an old man to crochet, but would be entirely wrong for a young man to have such a hobby."[25]

Frances's younger cousin, Isabel F. Harmon, remembers Preston as a "delightful man." "I think they had a happy life together," she wrote. "Dr. Preston has been a guest at our house and we enjoyed him, a witty, companionable, clever man."[26]

Years later, Francis Grover Cleveland, who, as the youngest of the Cleveland children, had reason to resent Preston the most, told his biographer, "[S]ome thought that Preston did not treat [my mother] as a First Lady should be treated, but by the same token [I] heard others suggest that perhaps she married him because he did not put her on a pedestal."[27]

Preston loved fast cars and, unlike Cleveland, had a strong interest in clothes. The Wells students called him a "classy dresser," having counted twenty-eight different suits in which he had appeared in Aurora.[28]

Frances welcomed the change that her new marriage created. A full-page photograph in the March 1913 *Harper's Bazaar* portrays a couple who look as if they have come directly off the pages of F. Scott Fitzgerald's *The Great Gatsby*. Posing beside their roadster, Preston looks dapper in his dark suit, and Frances looks bridal in her white, tailored jacket and skirt.

Her letter to Helena Gilder reflected the apparent optimism:

We will have been married a month tomorrow.

Sometimes I wonder if the theory of our complete physical change every seven years may not be true. It seems so remarkable to me that the person I am—or

was—should find it so perfectly natural & so satisfying to
be married—to have been married for a whole month to
a man who was never any part of all my old life. When I
regard myself objectively I can hardly comprehend it—but
I know I am very happy & peaceful. I am eager to have
you know Tom Preston. I feel sure you will come to it
with mind completely unbiased & that you will find
the rare spirit that I have found there—from some it is
almost completely hidden by a sort of defense of pride
& shyness combined.[29]

Preston had to adjust to living in the shadow of the "former Mrs.
Grover Cleveland," as Frances was typically referred to in newspaper
accounts throughout the remainder of her life. That shadow loomed
large immediately after the Prestons returned from their Florida
honeymoon. Frances, together with her children Richard, Esther, and
Marion, attended ceremonies at Cleveland's birthplace, in Caldwell,
New Jersey. The manse, adjacent to the First Presbyterian Church, was
purchased by the Grover Cleveland Birthplace Memorial Association.
The association took possession of the title to the property on the
seventy-sixth anniversary of Cleveland's birth. Preston was not listed
as one of the attendees.[30]

The marriage changed Frances in another way: she became openly
political. The voices demanding suffrage for women were becoming
louder, but there was an answering chord from women who were
antisuffrage. Frances was elected a vice president of the New Jersey
Association Opposed to Woman's Suffrage in May 1913.[31] She held
the post until the Nineteenth Amendment, granting women the right
to vote, was ratified on August 26, 1920.

Frances's position echoed Cleveland's strong antisuffrage views,
and reflected Frances's own beliefs. Antisuffragists considered the call
for suffrage part of a larger movement to change radically the social
order so that women would no longer be in charge of their own
sphere. They found fault with even the smallest changes in established
social practices, such as criticizing women who no longer used their
husband's names on their calling cards, preferring to be identified by
their own names. Such practices were viewed as an affront to the men
who provided the financial support for women and their children.

Antisuffragists believed that politics should remain the purview of men, and that women's votes were unnecessary.

A broadside published by the Anti-Suffrage Association proclaimed, "[S]uffrage is to be regarded not as a privilege to be enjoyed, but as a duty to be performed; . . . hitherto the women of this State have enjoyed exemption from this burdensome duty, and no adequate reason has been assigned for depriving them of that immunity; . . . the energies of women are engrossed by their present duties and interests, from which men cannot relieve them, and it is better for the community that they devote their energies to the more efficient performance of their present work than to divert them to new fields of activity." The most telling statement was this: "[P]olitical equality will deprive women of special privileges hitherto accorded to her by law.[32]

In her position as an officer of the New Jersey Association for Anti-Suffrage, Frances asserted these ideas, even while she continued to work on behalf of educational opportunities for all women and fair employment opportunities for unmarried women.

The contrast between Frances's views and her works represents the tension within America about the role and rights of women. Those who supported suffrage and equality under the law were driven by a desire to protect women from the abuses of a system that often treated women as second-class citizens—or worse, as children. As late as the early 1900s, women in many states were unable to obtain full legal status to enter into contracts, receive inheritances, or seek a divorce. Frances's devotion to the education of women was driven by her belief that they would be better wives and mothers. However, that same educational attainment paved the way for women to demand full-fledged citizenship in every area of American life, ranging from the ballot box to the boardroom.

Frances's White House years made her painfully aware of the struggles that many women faced. Her mail had been full of letters from destitute widows, mothers, and wives of disabled men seeking economic relief from their penury. Frances's worldview made accommodation for women who needed employment, but she never fully accepted that economic independence and suffrage were logical consequences of equal educational opportunities.

This latter view was one that Frances continued to hold, even after she exercised her own right to vote. In an interview in 1932, she assured her listeners that while she dutifully cast her ballot, it really was not necessary that women have that right.[33]

She did, however, continue to be noticeably political. In 1928, she openly demonstrated her support for the Democrats' Catholic presidential candidate, Alfred E. Smith, the target of strong anti-Catholic attacks, by sitting with Mrs. Smith at rallies for the candidate.[34]

Frances expressed her opinion about Franklin Roosevelt, too. "We were all Democrats," noted her youngest son, Francis, in a 1984 interview.

> But when Franklin Roosevelt ran for a third term, in 1940, my mother wouldn't vote for him. She said, "Your father never approved of a third term."
>
> Four years later, she voted for Roosevelt. She told me, "Your father never said anything about a fourth term."[35]

# *11*

# "America is simply not used to being serious about anything"

On March 16, 1914, Frances wrote to Helena: "Esther & Francis are going with us to England first, then Holland & Belgium & later Italy. We talk of six months & don't know what the future holds beyond that."[1]

Frances's last statement turned out to be prophetic. Four months later, a Serbian extremist, Gavilo Princip, assassinated the Austrian archduke Franz Ferdinand and his wife, Duchess Sophie, on June 28, 1914. Most expatriate Americans considered the incident an inconsequential local matter. But the murder of the Austrian ruler exacerbated already rising tensions within central Europe. Czarist Russia, facing increasing pressures from a growing Bolshevik movement, flexed its muscles on behalf of Serbia, one of its client states, and warned Austria that it would not permit it to embarrass Serbia. Austria's response was to blame the Serbian government for what it called "pan-Slav agitation." By July 25, after nearly a month of increasingly vitriolic rhetoric, it was clear that battle lines were drawn.[2]

Frances's gossipy letter to Helena in early July gives no hint of the war clouds gathering ominously over Europe. Instead, it presents an enlightening picture of Frances's many social connections, Esther's growing affinity for British life, Preston's separate travels, and Emma's declining health.

July 8, 1914
Whitehall, Bloomsbury Square, London
Dearest Helena,

I dined night before last at the House of Commons with a Conservative member & had a long talk after dinner on the Terrace in the light of the full moon—with Sir. Chas Waldstein & we went back to the old Marion days & to you & your Richard & many good old common friends. Not a day passes but I do see friends of yours, but this talk brought you especially near. I have not heard a word of you in any way since I hurried off from your tea table to catch my steamer. I suppose of course you are in the country by now. I miss it so & I did enjoy the glimpse of hills I had ten days ago with Adele when we went to Broadwer & had tea with Miss Maria Wedgewood (where we *did* talk of you!) & spent the night at Mr. Millet's house through the —— in London. We called on the Locherns who have a house there, now & Mary de Navarro & next day motored to Gloucester—stopping also at Tewkesbury. It is the only trip away I have taken. I was afraid Esther would be too dull in the country, though we were tempted to take a little place some where for a month. But we have been busy every moment. Mother & Marion came Saturday & now we are still here waiting for Richard who sailed yesterday I suppose & then we plan to go to St. Moritz. Mother is not very well. She has some sort of digestive trouble I think. Our Princeton doctor seemed to think it was that. She had been so well up to the time I was at home in May—and that Sunday she was faint in church & hasn't felt really right since but I hope she will improve over here.

Give much love to the girls and boys! & do send me a line at least. I want to know how your summer is going. Address me at the Kulm—St. Moritz—or else at American Express, London.

Devotedly ever,
Frank
My love to Rosamond! Marion was *nineteen* yesterday.[3]

Three weeks later, Europe was at war. France, Great Britain, and Russia declared hostilities against Germany.

For the large number of Americans who typically spent summers in Europe, the outbreak of war created an entirely unexpected level of uncertainty and hardship. Bank moratoriums in London and Paris made it difficult for Americans to get the needed funds to purchase tickets and return home. London quickly became the most popular spot of embarkation, and Americans flocked to that city, filling hotels to overflowing.

Frances's friends in the United States were obviously worried about the well-being of the family, and Frank Hastings, Frances's business manager, wrote to Mrs. Daniel Lamont at the end of August as soon as he had heard from Frances.

August 31, 1914
My dear Mrs. Lamont:
   After a long silence I have just had a letter from Mrs. Preston. Her mail address is: Hotel Engadiner Klum, St. Moritz, Engadine, Switzerland. She asked me to communicate with you and say that the mail facilities are few and far between and that she had only time to write me a hurried letter on business. They are all well excepting her mother, who is confined to her room a large part of the time with some muscular affliction of the heart. They have a very good local doctor, which they like very much, and Mrs. Preston says they are quite content to stay where they are for the present, and even if they had an opportunity she hardly feels that her mother is well enough to come away at the present time. Doctor Preston is in Mannheim, Germany, with his mother and sister, and although they are unable to communicate with him since the war broke out, Frances says that she feels that she has no cause for worriment. Her four children of course are with her, and they are all well. She tells me that they are requested to be very careful of the food supply, although she adds that the food given them is plenty and of good quality. She has no difficulty in getting money under her Morgan credit, and in fact states that the Hotel will accept their checks on

their New York banks in payment of their board bill. The
Bissells, Hibbens, and Mr. Bartlett are there, beside some
"good old Buffalo friends." There is no sign of any panic
there although they are having difficulty in ascertaining
what is going on outside.

    With kind regards, believe me,
    Very sincerely yours,
    (Signed) F. S. Hastings[4]

A subsequent letter from Frances prompted Hastings to write
again, assuring friends of her family's well-being. Frances's typical
optimism and reassuring attitude conveys the sense that she and her
small group were virtually untouched by the disruptions to their travels. She drew more attention to her mother's illness as the reason for
their stay in Switzerland, and in describing her ailing mother Frances
used virtually the same language that she had used to describe the
declining health of Grover Cleveland. The letter from Hastings read
as follows:

September 3, 1914
Memo Re Mrs. Thomas J. Preston, Jr.
    I have just received a letter from Mrs. Preston dated
August 18th and she was then in St. Moritz with her Mother
and four children and was unable to leave on account of
her Mother's serious illness which she describes as being
due to intestinal poisoning. She has the services of a good
nurse from the Presbyterian Hospital of New York and also
an excellent Swiss Doctor. Mrs. Preston states that they are
very comfortable and that although cautioned about the
scarcity of food they still have plenty to eat of excellent
quality. The Hibbens and Bissells and a number of other
friends were still there. Dr. Preston was at Eisenach with
his Mother and sister but could not get out of Germany.
She says that she is able to get money in small quantities
and that the hotel people are taking her checks on New
York in payment of her board.
    The New York Times of this morning states that
Mrs. Preston is leaving St. Moritz with her children. This
however I very much doubt, because, under date of August

18th she states that it would be impossible for her to leave
there for some time to come on account of her Mother's
continued ill health.

Very sincerely yours,

F. S. Hastings[5]

A short time later, Hastings sent word that Frances and her family,
minus Preston, had been able to secure passage and leave Europe:

A cable received from Mrs. Preston, dated, Zurich, September 8th, states that they are leaving Genoa, September
17th, by the Steamer 'Tomasso Di Savoia.' This is one of
the Italian Line, running to Buenos Aires, and I understand
it is a very fine and comfortable ship. I am without any
knowledge as to the whereabouts of Dr. Preston. Although
it is possible that he may be coming with them. I doubt it
very much, as the last I heard of him was in Mannheim,
Germany.

F. S. Hastings[6]

The shipped docked in New York on October 1.[7] By October
5, Frances was writing a cheerful note to Helena:

We are safely home! Mother is very much better, in fact
well—though not quite strong. We are camping out in the
Princeton Inn for a month. I expect Tom Preston the 17th
on the Mauretania. We got separated going different ways
with our invalid mothers and had to come home different
routes. We had no hardships nor inconveniences beyond
being obliged to return on an Italian ship taking two weeks
but it was clean & quite comfortable. I hope to see you
soon. I am in town for a few hours—let me know when
you are coming down. Dear love to you all.

Devotedly,

Frank[8]

Frances's upbeat tone belied a hair-raising story that Preston told
several years later regarding his situation when the war started. In a
speech made at a New York church in March 1918, Preston told the

audience that he had been studying ancient Latin and Greek manu-
scripts in Nauheim, Germany, when war was declared.

> I was arrested, [Preston told the group], with seven other
> men, and taken before a military official in a fortress in
> Nauheim. The other prisoners, whose nationalities I did not
> learn, were struck in the face, knocked down and brutally
> kicked. I attribute the fact that I was not similarly handled
> to the slightly better clothes that I wore. The official asked
> me if I had a passport, and when I told him that I had
> one [but not with me], he cursed me and said he was
> convinced that I was a British spy. He said that unless I
> could procure a passport in five days, I needn't bother to
> try, for it would do me no good.
>
> They marched me to a cell, and every day while I was
> there I would hear at least once a volley of shots, and the
> guard would come by, laughing, and tell me that my turn
> would come soon. Thanks to the efforts of my relatives and
> Ambassador Gerard the passport arrived in time.[9]

Preston's firsthand experiences at the hands of Germans as
enemies may have been the catalyst for the couple's involvement in
the National Security League (NSL), an organization founded by
S. Stanwood Menken.

Menken, a highly respected New York corporate attorney who
represented some of the largest corporations in America, formed the
league to promote war preparedness in a nation that was still very
much isolationist.

Menken had been conducting business in Europe on behalf of
his clients when the war started. At its outbreak, Menken worked
with future president Herbert Hoover to assist in securing the safe
return of over ninety thousand Americans. He helped locate shelter
and funds while these war refugees waited for a way to return home,
and, at Mrs. Hoover's suggestion, Menken edited a small newspaper
that published the embarkation schedules. Menken's experiences led
to the development of his ideas regarding American war preparedness
and the organization that became the league.[10]

The Prestons became active in the league through their friendship with Robert McElroy, a noted professor of history at Princeton.

In 1917, when the United States formally entered the war, the NSL formed the Committee on Patriotism through Education. The committee organized educators and secured speakers who would deliver "win the war" speeches at educational institutions throughout the country.[11] McElroy headed the committee, and he asked Preston to become director of the committee's Speakers' Bureau. Frances served on the Executive Committee.

Although McElroy was the chief catalyst in securing the Prestons' involvement in the league, the Prestons had other connections with Menken. The couple maintained friendships with former presidents Roosevelt and Taft, who were friends of Menken. Roosevelt and Rodman Gilder, who had taken over the publication of *Century Magazine* following his father's death, worked closely with Menken during the NSL's early years.

Gilder served on the board, and Roosevelt made speeches nationwide in support of the United States's preparedness and involvement in the war.[12]

The Prestons' affiliation with the National Security League was a curious one. They and the Woodrow Wilsons were the only two Democratic families in Princeton during the years prior to Wilson becoming president of the United States in 1913. Menken, a Democrat himself, also knew Wilson well. However, Wilson did not share the views of the league, and was resistant to its call for preparedness.

Menken found stronger support for his preparedness views among Republicans. The Prestons found themselves more aligned with Republicans like Roosevelt and Taft on this issue. In one note to Frances, Roosevelt had written, "You sound like a Republican."[13]

Frances was the first woman to become a member of the league's Executive Committee, and she threw herself into the committee's activities with her typical enthusiasm. "There is a great need now to educate the people in the why and wherefore of the war," she told reporters. "That is the only way toward gaining a worthwhile and active patriotism." Echoing language that was typical of McElroy, she continued, "The apathy surrounding an appreciable proportion of the nation is due not so much to conscious unwillingness to help, but to a lack of appreciation of the things we are fighting for."[14]

Frances replaced her husband as secretary of the Committee on Patriotism through Education, in late 1918. Preston had resigned his position as secretary to assume the presidency of the New York

Homeopathic Medical College and Flowers Hospital. By then, however, her title was an acknowledgment of the leadership she had exerted on behalf of the committee throughout the year.[15]

Part of that leadership put her in the position of having to defend McElroy. McElroy held unequivocal views on patriotism, and as the war dragged on, he abandoned his historian's objectivity in favor of stronger, often incendiary, language. In April 1918, McElroy spoke to a campus gathering of ten thousand Liberty Loan marchers at the University of Wisconsin. The weather was cold and rainy, and by the time McElroy, who was the day's last speaker, reached the podium, the audience was wet and shivering.

Tired and cold, many of the marchers left before the end of the speeches. The remaining audience consisted primarily of student cadets, who were soaked and freezing themselves. "During this ordeal the cadets grew restless," one observer noted, "some clicking their rifles and others 'schishing' to quiet them. This distraction, coupled with his loss of audience, infuriated McElroy. He boomed, "By God, I believe you are traitors!" The historian Carl Russell Fish spent that afternoon trying to convince McElroy of his error without success.[16]

The university's reaction was swift and furious. The school's president demanded an apology from McElroy and the NSL. Menken replied with a mild defense of McElroy's account of the events. The debate continued into May. Students paraded through the community carrying two effigies: one of the kaiser, labeled "Me und Gott"; the other of McElroy, reading "McNutts, Prince of Asses." Both effigies were burned on the campus quadrangle.

Kathleen Burke, a Wisconsin member of the NSL, telegraphed Theodore Roosevelt and Frances with her account of McElroy's speech. Her report included this description:

> I do not believe the whole audience was hostile but there were groups in various sections of the hall who appeared to deliberately make noise or to behave in such a manner as to distract the rest of the audience, besides clicking bayonets, whispering behind caps, one group had a dog which they passed from man to man, held up in the air, etc., etc., which as a stranger it would not be right for me to express an opinion as to the patriotism of the audience.

I can confirm the following facts—the speaker [McElroy]
stepped to the edge of the platform and said in a voice
loud enough to be heard at the end of the hall, that he
had often wondered how he would feel when speaking
before a hostile audience, and he believed the audience to
be sixty percent blank Prussians. I was fully prepared to
see the audience rise en masse to deny the statement, but
it only caused a kind of half sneer or smile throughout
the audience, the denial should certainly have been made
then and there. . . .[17]

Frances included a letter of her own, typed on NSL letterhead,
with another copy of the telegram to Roosevelt. In it she again confirmed the NSL's support of McElroy's version of the events:

Dr. McElroy claims he said to that audience that he believed
a part of them were traitors owing to the manner in which
they acted at the time he was reading portions of President
Wilson's message. . . . Their position is that Dr. McElroy never
said what he claimed and they also claim after his return
from his speaking trip, Dr. McElroy maliciously stated that
the University and State of Wisconsin were disloyal. With
regard to this, Dr. McElroy specially mentioned that he
congratulated the State of Wisconsin on its loyalty as a result
of which they had elected Senator Lenroot and also spoke in
the same general terms of the loyalty of the University.
   It is absolutely ridiculous to suppose that Dr. McElroy
would characterize a whole state or an institution in this
wholesale fashion with disloyalty, as he has been particularly
careful not to make any statement for which governmental
authority could not be obtained. . . .
   At a meeting of the Executive Committee of this
League, held on the afternoon of Friday, May 17th,
Dr. McElroy's position was unanimously upheld by the
Board. . . .[18]

The McElroy issue highlighted another, more pressing issue
for the NSL: support for Menken as the organization's president.

Menken and the newspaper magnate William Randolph Hearst had enjoyed a good working relationship since the founding of the NSL in 1915. Hearst had allotted favorable editorial and news coverage to the organization's views. In turn, the organization accepted his support without criticizing Hearst's obvious Anglophobic stance in his paper's editorials. (Most of the NSL's board and active membership were very pro-England.)

In the wake of the McElroy-Wisconsin issue, Hearst encountered Menken in New York's Palace Hotel. A month had already elapsed since the April incident, but Hearst complained to Menken that McElroy's remarks were "intemperate." Menken replied that his educational director had overreached himself. Hearst asked Menken if he would put those comments in writing, and the following morning, Menken did so.[19]

Publication of Menken's comments caused a firestorm within the NSL. The Prestons, as well as the entire Speakers' Bureau, threatened to leave the organization. Elihu Root, a key Republican leader and chair of the board of the Carnegie Corporation, backed the Prestons' ultimatum. Writing to Roosevelt on the eve of the NSL board's June 25 meeting, Frances commented, "I have brought my youngest boy up here to spend a short time near Marion. I go to NY tonight for the fateful meeting of the Nat. Security League tomorrow. If Mr. Menken remains as President of the Board, I don't see how Mr. Preston and I can stay on."[20]

The Prestons did not need to worry. Root threatened to withdraw Carnegie Corporation's considerable financial support of the NSL if Menken remained as president. The potential loss of $100,000 in income to the organization spoke louder than any oratory. Of the fifty-two members of the NSL's Executive Committee who voted at the meeting, only seven supported Menken.[21]

The McElroy/Menken brouhaha did not prevent Frances from being uncharacteristically vocal and visible in her pro-war activities. Unlike Grover Cleveland, who was adamant that wives—including his—should be seen and not heard, Thomas Preston apparently had no difficulty with an openly opinionated, outspoken spouse.

A speech made to a packed crowd at New York's Carnegie Hall echoed the themes that characterized Frances's life: duty and sacrifice, commitment to family, and the value of motherhood. There is also the echo of her religious commitment, as she exhorted the crowd to have a "steadfast purpose."

"The bravest battle that was ever fought was fought by the mothers of men," she told the attendees at the war rally.

> Today, we mothers and wives of the soldiers of Freedom, face the old grim fact of war; but this is a war to end war; and therefore our eyes must be dry and our hearts unswerving for sacrifice. More than that, we must all serve. Not grief but labor, not tears, but steadfast purpose, are worthy of the men who bear our colors against the enemy of the world's peace. Above all we must let our soldiers know that the women of America are behind them, steadfast, resolute, and demanding the victory which alone can bring disarmament and a lasting peace.[22]

Steadfastness continued to be Frances's theme as she made speeches throughout the country during 1918. "We can win if America can be held steadfast and unswerving, and the women of America can hold steadfast," she wrote in a message that was addressed to the "women of America" and distributed by the NSL. "Liberty is not safe. It is menaced along the battlefront of many nations, our own among them, and America requires a new motto for her old bell: 'Proclaim liberty throughout all the inhabitants thereof.' Until liberty is safe in all lands, it cannot be safe in our own. Hence the task to which America has reverently and unselfishly dedicated herself."[23]

By the November 1918 election, the Prestons had abandoned the NSL. Their decision was timely. A congressional investigation, convened by the new Congress in 1919, sought to discredit the organization based on the NSL's alleged harassment of congressional incumbents whom it had targeted as "unpatriotic."[24]

One historian summed up the activities of the NSL this way: "It had turned from its original advocacy of preparedness, and using the intolerance and conformity of war which it had helped to foster, had sought to imbue the interests that it represented with a public sanctity. In so doing, it had failed to heed all of Theodore Roosevelt's dictum that 'everything is un-American that tends either to government by a plutocracy, or government by a mob.' "[25]

Frances's interest in the prosecution of the war was not merely an intellectual exercise. Esther had traveled to England to perform volunteer work in 1917, and she was assigned to the St. Dunstan's Home for Blind Soldiers, in London. There she became reacquainted with William Sidney Bence Bosanquet, a British soldier whom she had met two years previously, in Switzerland. The couple married in a quiet ceremony in Westminster Abbey in March 1918.[26]

There were other changes in Frances's family. Esther's younger sister, Marion, had wed William Stanley Dell on November 28, 1917.[27] Richard enlisted in the Marines on June 18, 1918, the "tenth anniversary of his father's death," Frances wrote Theodore Roosevelt.[28] Francis, who was only fifteen years old, was away at school most of the year. Frances's children had grown and left home.

As the peace process took shape, Frances continued to press her point of view. Former president William Howard Taft, who had avoided involvement in the NSL but had headed his own organization, the League to Enforce Peace, formed a committee of influential women to participate in a campaign to strengthen women's opposition to a premature and indecisive peace. Frances, in her position as secretary of the National Security League's Committee on Patriotism through Education, served on that committee. The chair of the committee, also appointed by Taft, was Dr. Anna Shaw, honorary president of the National American Woman's Suffrage Association.[29]

Frances spoke to the delegates to the National Service Congress Convention, meeting in Chicago in February 1918. Former president Taft had already addressed the group, cautioning against a hasty, and inconclusive, peace. Frances's words had the tone and message of Grover Cleveland when she charged that

> the women of America are not working together sufficiently to win the war and until they do it will never be won.
>
> If they could only realize that this war is not 3,000 miles away, but is a dreadful shadow that is altogether too near and that it will affect them as well as their children, they would be like-minded about this conflict.

Then, using McElroy-like language, she added, "America is simply not used to being serious about anything, and it will take the casualty lists to make women realize the enormity of the problem. I believe that is due to the fact that there is a huge percentage of unassimilated population that cannot think or act together."[30]

Frances's temperance views also found their way into her support for the war effort. At the end of February 1918, as the battle to ban the manufacture and sale of alcohol was making its way to the floor of Congress, nearly six million women, including Frances, presented President Wilson with a petition urging that "the production of malt liquors in the United States be stopped in the interest of the conservation of foodstuffs.

"The petition states," reported the *New York Times*, "that the grain being used in the brewing of beer, ale and other malt beverages in America is enough to make more than 4,000,000 loaves of bread daily, and that the women of America ask that this great saving be made by a proclamation of the President."[31]

Frances's name was still mentioned in the press as the women's war organizations found themselves embroiled in petty controversies as the peace process ground on through late 1918 and early 1919. The president of the National Association Opposed to Woman Suffrage, Mrs. James W. Wadsworth, Jr., sent a letter to all of the nation's organizations of women, urging that only those who opposed suffrage be appointed to the American delegation at the peace conference.

Her intent was allegedly to discredit three active suffragists: Carrie Chapman Catt, Dr. Anna Howard Shaw, and Jane Addams. These three women were viewed as pacifists, and it was believed that they would have a negative impact on the terms imposed on the Central Powers at the peace conference.

Mrs. Wadsworth did support the participation of her fellow antisuffragist Frances Cleveland Preston. She said, "If it were suggested that Mrs. Thomas J. Preston, Jr., whom ex-president Taft, a political opponent of her former husband, calls 'the most beloved woman in America,' be appointed on the peace commission because of her distinguished service with the League to Enforce Peace and the National Security League, this organization would be the last to raise objection . . . because we feel that [she] would serve [her] country first and not enter into a compact to serve a political cause first."[32]

Frances's activities in the NSL were out of step with all that had previously characterized her life. During her White House years, she had embraced minorities, lower-income people, and people of lesser educational backgrounds. Most of her children's nurses and nannies were of Germanic or Scandinavian descent. Frances had studied German in order to become fluent in the language. The organizations in which Frances was active—the Needlework Guild, the New York Kindergarten Association, and the Presbyterian Home Mission Board—were committed to meeting the needs of the underprivileged while upholding their dignity as human beings.

It is a matter of pure speculation as to what led both her and Preston to become involved in the league. The social relationship that the couple had with the Roosevelts and with the Tafts certainly would have been a strong influence. More than likely, McElroy, a close Princeton friend, was the catalyst that moved both of them into the NSL's inner circle.

By the close of 1919, Frances was once again out of the limelight. The war had ended. She and Tom had abandoned their activities with the National Security League. And the America that Frances knew was changing: women had attained the constitutional right to vote, and all Americans were constitutionally denied the right to buy alcohol.

# 12

# "I wish only a true picture of his life"

Frances's mother, Emma Folsom Perrine, died on December 26, 1915, fourteen months after she returned from war-torn Europe.[1] From the time of Oscar Folsom's premature death until the time of her own, Emma had been a mainstay in her daughter's life. While there had been periods of tension between the two women, the love and care for each other prevailed, as Frances indicated in a letter to Helena Gilder:

> . . . I shall miss exercise [the Preston's were on Commodore Benedict's boat, *Oneida*, and bound for Cuba]—but perhaps the freedom from all exertion will be good for me for a while & one must adjust one's self to new situations. Why should it be any different from having my mother even thousands of miles away but it is—it is that I have lost my chance to do for her—she was so dear—so gentle—so contented & satisfied this last year & so amazingly well & strong in every way—& she had her child and grandchildren around her—she was not ill long—she must have suffered little if any physical pain & she just fell asleep like a little child at the end. It came like a great peace-giver.
>
> She had such a powerful personality—with all her tenderness—that we miss her everywhere.[2]

Five months later, Frances lost Helena Gilder, who died on May 28, 1916, after an operation for appendicitis.[3] Helena's death represented another link dropped from the chain of Frances and Grover Cleveland's shared lives.

New relationships transformed other links in that chain. The friendship that had started between the Clevelands and John and Martha Finley survived and thrived after Frances's remarriage to Thomas Preston. Preston became a part of this foursome, bringing with him his outstanding skills as a pianist. He played for the family religious services that were held on Sunday evenings in the summer months when both families were in residence.

As World War I drew to a close, Frances took the lead in preserving Grover Cleveland's legacy. In 1919, she authorized Robert McElroy to write the first comprehensive biography of the late president, offering her full cooperation in the effort together with her ideas for the project.

> December 28, 1919
> Princeton, New Jersey
> 　　Mr. Dear Dr. McElroy:
> 　　I am delighted to hear that you have arranged with Harper and Brothers for the publication of the authorized biography of Mr. Cleveland.
> 　　Your plan to use some of the material in Harper's Magazine before publishing the book seems to me very wise. Although you are writing a biography from original and hitherto unused sources, your aim, I know, is to reach the people as well as the special student of history, and I fully sympathise with that desire. Mr. Cleveland's heart was always with "the people"; his thought was always for "the people"; and it is to them that any true picture of his life will make the strongest appeal.
> 　　I have turned over to you all of his papers, without reservations and without conditions. I wish only a true picture of his life.
> 　　Very sincerely yours,
> 　　Frances F. Cleveland Preston[4]

Frances's choice of biographer did not meet with approval from all of Cleveland's former associates. William Gorham Rice responded to Frances's letter asking his assistance in working with McElroy, and he expressed clear disappointment in her choice.

> My doubt about pledging myself to joint work did not particularly refer to Mr. McElroy, whom I know slightly, but applied equally to any one else but Dr. Finley. What lines of possible cooperation would follow only personal conference could determine.
>
> I had looked forward with great pleasure to association in this work with Dr. Finley. And while I am happy that the definitive life is now to go forward to completion I am regretful that he [Finley] has not felt able to devote himself to it.[5]

Finley never wrote a biography of Cleveland, but, as president of the Cleveland Birthplace Association, he supported the Columbia University history professor Allan Nevins in his work on Cleveland that was published in 1932. Nevins won a Pulitzer Prize for his biography of the president, and became another spokesperson for Cleveland's courage and independence. At the ninety-fifth anniversary of Cleveland's birth, Nevins told the assembled group, which included Frances, "[T]he one quality that made him great, his unyielding moral courage, could never have existed as it did but for his fine consciousness, his warm sensibility and his innate religious feeling. These were the hidden springs which fed his hard-fighting power."[6]

In conjunction with her choice of collaboration with McElroy, Frances chose the Library of Congress as the repository for Cleveland's massive body of correspondence. Cleveland had been a prolific letter writer, and had maintained an ongoing correspondence with hundreds of influential people across nearly a half century of friendships and public life. Frances undertook the monumental task of writing letters to every one of Cleveland's cabinet members or their heirs, all of his close friends, and most of his business associates. Her letter reflects her understanding of history and the importance of maintaining the documents that represented Cleveland's presidency.

An example of her attitude is found in the letter written to Mrs. Henry Vilas, the wife of Cleveland's postmaster general during Cleveland's second administration:

> After very careful consideration I have decided that in so far as I can gain the consent of the owners [of the letters sent to McElroy for work on the biography] I shall turn these papers over to the Library of Congress. There they will receive excellent care and be made easily available for the use of scholars from every part of the world. No library in this country has equal facilities for the effective use of collections of this character. If kept together, these papers will make easy the work of future students of the period during which Mr. Cleveland was active in public affairs, but if once dispersed it will be practically impossible ever to get them together again.[7]

The vast majority of those whom Frances contacted were willing to have their letters deposited in the Library of Congress. Margaret Bissell, who was the daughter of the Clevelands' close Buffalo friends the Wilson Bissells, and who had been a White House playmate of Ruth's when her father was postmaster general, enthusiastically endorsed Frances's plan:

> Dearest Cousin Frances:
>     Your letter has caught up with us here, and I hasten to reply in writing what I said in Princeton—that I think your idea about keeping the letters together in the Library of Congress is the right one, and I shall be glad to leave the letters which were written to my father with the others. I can't remember ever hearing Mother make any suggestions as to their future, but I know that you and she usually felt the same about everything, and I know that she would want to cooperate with you.
>     . . . Burnham [Margaret's husband and a relation of Marion Cleveland's husband] had a long and most delightful letter from Stanley this morning—full of cheer and enthusiasm.

With love to you all,
Affectionately,
Margaret B. Dell[8]

However, not everyone was willing to comply with Frances's request. Mr. James F. Tracey, of Albany, New York, wrote on his wife's behalf that she wished to retain her letters from Cleveland.

Frances, in her typically gracious style, replied:

My dear Mr. Tracey:
    I wish to thank you for your kind letter of June 28th. I, of course, do not wish to insist upon the sugges- tion which I made regarding Mrs. Tracey's collection of Mr. Cleveland's letters, and fully appreciate her reasons for desiring to retain them. In allowing Dr. McElroy to use them in the preparation of the Biography she has done us a great service, and it would be ungrateful of me to ask any further sacrifice.
    I am very sorry indeed to hear of Mrs. Tracey's illness, and hope that she will soon be restored to perfect health.[9]

The one ongoing constant in Frances's life was what she called her "charity work." While organizing speakers for the National Security League, Frances continued her involvement in the Needlework Guild of America. The guild, which was started in the United States in 1884, was modeled after a European organization that had its roots in England. Lady Wolverton, a clergyman's daughter, recognized the need for good, homemade clothing, and she began an organization that would provide handmade garments for those in need.

In America, the guild reached into all levels of society. "It is not, as might be inferred from the wealth and social position of many of its officers, a 'fashionable charity,' " noted an article in *Harper's Bazaar*. "On the contrary, it knows neither race, color, sect, nor condition of servitude in its membership, which extends from the Atlantic to the Pacific."[10]

Frances first became active in the guild in 1896, when, as first lady, she made a layette outfit for a poor black girl who only had

rags for her infant. During the war, Frances's relationship deepened
with Theodore Roosevelt's wife, Edith, who had joined the guild at
Frances's suggestion. "Mrs. Preston and Mrs. Roosevelt have a common enthusiasm in the Needlework Guild of America, which is a
major welfare activity of both of them. . . . Mrs. Preston is national
president of the Guild. Roosevelt once told his wife that he knew of
no other organization in the United States which did so much good
with so little fuss as the Guild."[11]

In her fifteen years as the national president, Frances extended
the guild's influence into other organizations. In 1925, she was
appointed to the board of directors of the Camp Fire Girls.[12] Needlework Guild projects continued to be a part of the Camp Fire Girls
experience as late as 1959.[13] In 1939, the girls' organization was a
part of the junior guild, and participated in the making of clothing
that was contributed to the Labrador mission of Sir Winfred Grenfell.
Frances had developed a friendship with Grenfell through Martha
Finley, whose son-in-law, while an undergraduate at Yale University,
had worked with the Labrador missionary. The women regularly
supported Grenfell's work among the impoverished local population
in Labrador, and Frances, in her position as president of the guild,
organized the delivery of thousands of garments to Labrador and
northern Newfoundland.[14]

When interviewed, Frances often used the attention given to
the guild's national convention to promote her views. In 1932, while
visiting Asheville, North Carolina, she said, "I don't think we should
discuss this depression so much. . . . [T]here has been nothing to
compare with it in my lifetime. . . . This depression touches the very
heart of our country and I do not believe that there has ever been
such a converging of varied problems as we have now. All I can do
is make a guess about the outcome, just like anybody else does. We
can only do our best."[15]

Age did not change Frances's views about a woman's role. She
continued to be an antisuffragist, maintaining that "she has never been
able to see that woman's right to vote has solved any problems, nor
brought about any reforms that could not have been brought about
anyway through the natural evolution of time."[16]

She also continued to hold the view that women should only
work out of absolute economic necessity. "Women in business?" she

asked, in response to a question. "Yes, there are some women who should be in business, but there are many working now whom I believe should not occupy these positions. There are so many girls and women, if not wealthy, who are well-to-do, who occupy positions now which should be occupied by other persons who need them more, and upon whom others are dependent."[17]

Frances resigned as national president of the guild in 1939, at the age of seventy-five. During her tenure, she had overseen the annual collection and distribution of millions of garments across the country. In 1938 alone, the guild had provided over two million pieces of clothing to people in need.[18]

Frances maintained her seat as a trustee of Wells College for forty years. She was entering her thirty-sixth year of service when she agreed to lead the college's Million Dollar Campaign. The campaign was launched in March 1922, with national headquarters in New York City. Each alumna was assigned a quota of $333 "to get or give," payable over five years. Several brochures and well-illustrated pamphlets came out, presenting life at Wells College past and present. The alumnae organized dinners and fund-raising events. By June 1922 more than $700,000 had been raised from more than twenty-five hundred former students, both graduates and nongraduates, and 1924 saw the successful completion of the campaign.[19]

The end of World War I marked the renewal of Frances's worldwide travels, especially visits to the home in England of her daughter Esther, who was expecting a child. On October 8, 1920, Frances wrote to Mrs. M. S. Thomas, who was McElroy's administrative assistant and who assumed the responsibilities of handling the Prestons' personal correspondence in their absence. Frances's comment about the new baby's name is a poignant reminder of Ruth's absence from the family circle:

> After coming all this way to be with Esther in her hour of trial, I had gone to Cambridge to spend Sunday—when the baby came ten days ahead of scheduled time! She is a little darling and made very little disturbance or discomfort. We can't help being glad she is here instead of keeping us all waiting. All is going well. She is called Philippa Ruth, for her father's mother—and my oldest little girl—she

happened to be born on her birthday—so Esther and I have double pleasure in her having the name.[20]

In her typical style of attending to every detail, Frances also provided Mrs. Thomas with explicit instructions on handling correspondence:

> I forgot to ask you not to send the cancelled checks from the Banks, who generally make their statements on the 1st of the month. Please *do* send me the *statements*. . . .
>
> In the case of invitations for weddings—when to the *reception* please just *write* in the third person—on good paper—
>
> Mr. & Mrs. Preston regret that absence abroad will prevent their acceptance of ——, etc. Invitations to church only require an acknowledgment—let *teas* and *receptions* go—if there are any."[21]

A few weeks later, Frances, sounding as effusive as Emma had been about Frances' newborn children, wrote again about her new granddaughter to Mrs. Thomas: "Our new baby is a perfect little dear—I am enjoying this stage of her existence (two weeks old!) immensely. Her mother is fine and strong. She has already been down in the garden in the sunshine. The other baby is a perfect delight! I have quite full days. I manage to put in a good walk every day it is fine, and the weather has been quite wonderful, with a great deal of sunshine."[22]

She and Preston had traveled to Europe together, and Frances wrote that he continued on to Paris. She could not resist her educator's urge to correct Mrs. Thomas's spelling of the town where Esther lived. At the very end of the letter, below her signature, Frances wrote: "Owston—not Owsten!"

After spending the Thanksgiving and Christmas holidays of 1920 in New York and New Jersey, respectively, the Prestons traveled to Colorado Springs, Colorado, in midwinter, 1921, to visit Marion and her husband, Stanley Dell. Dell had a number of health problems, as alluded to in Margaret Bissell Dell's letter to Frances. Frances wrote to Mrs. Thomas:

All is well here. Mr. Dell is apparently progressing in a satisfactory manner. He seems perfectly well, but he is carrying
out his doctor's instructions and spending his nights and
most of his days out of doors and resting completely.

The baby [Marion's daughter, Frances, was her
grandmother's namesake] is adorable and a great diversion.
She is learning something new nearly every day.

Mrs. Dell is splendidly well. It is a joy to be with
them all, in this wonderful scenery and climate.[23]

The Finleys were active in the Young Women's Christian Association, and Frances was a member of its national board in 1922.
Her position gave her the opportunity to embark on a YWCA world
tour in the fall of 1922. They visited Japan; Hong Kong; Singapore;
Penang; Colombo and Kandy, Ceylon; and a variety of cities in India
and Egypt.[24]

Frances's letters to Mrs. Thomas tell little of what she experienced
on the tour, and instead contained an ongoing series of instructions
about what to do regarding correspondence, household accounts, and
messages. A typical letter, written aboard ship, reads: "Will you follow
the schedule sending c/o American Express to Cairo where we shall
get mail as late as April 5th—after that please address c/o American
Express—Naples, Italy (Piazza dei Martiri)? Please remember we are
using both Western Union and American Express Codes."[25]

Frances ended her voyage with a trip to England to visit her
daughter, Esther. Marion, together with her daughter, Frances, crossed
the Atlantic to be with her family. The Prestons had gone their separate
ways in Palestine, with Preston going on to Italy and France, while
Frances journeyed to England.[26]

Marion's visit without her husband, Stanley Dell, was evidence
that the marriage was not going well. Dell, who had been a journalist,
suffered from both real and imaginary health problems, which affected
his mental health. During World War I, he had been unable to enlist
in the Army, Navy, or Marine Corps due poor vision, although he
had been decorated for his work with the Red Cross in France.[27] The
couple's move out West was designed to help restore Dell to health,
but he continued to languish. Mention of Dell's health in Frances's

correspondence suggests that there was more to the situation than she was reporting.

When Marion's marriage ended in divorce, in 1926, Frances staunchly supported her daughter. While Frances held strong religious beliefs about abstention from alcohol and strict observance of the Sabbath, she was no stranger to divorce. Frances's aunt had obtained a divorce from her abusive husband over forty years earlier. "Now that the news is out," she told reporters, "I want it made clear that desertion constituted the ground for divorce. . . . desertion in the legal acceptance of the term. There is nothing further to say."[28]

On July 25, 1926, Marion married John Harlan Amen, who had been Richard Cleveland's roommate at Exeter Academy, in a ceremony that took place at the Clevelands' New Hampshire home, Intermont. Preston gave her in marriage. The couple had a son, Grover Cleveland Amen, and the senior Harlan became a prosecutor for the United States in the Nuremberg war crime trials held at the close of World War II. Like her mother, Marion devoted her efforts to organizations that supported young women, and she eventually worked for the Girl Scouts of America as a volunteer coordinator.

The early and mid-1920s was a season of weddings. On June 20, 1923, Richard married Ellen Douglass Gailor. She was the daughter of the then-presiding bishop of the Episcopal Church, Thomas Gailor. The couple settled in Baltimore, where Richard had established his law practice, and they had three children. That marriage ended in divorce in 1940, falling victim to Ellen's alcoholism. Richard married Jessie Maxwell Black on March 12, 1943. Jessie, like Frances, was considerably younger than her husband. Jessie and Richard had three children.[29]

Exactly two years after Richard and Ellen Gailor wed, Francis married Alice Erdman, daughter of a noted Presbyterian scholar, Reverend Dr. Charles Erdman, on June 20, 1925.[30] Francis, who inherited his mother's love of the theater, became an actor and the founder of the Barnstormers, a professional summer theater group that he operated out of the family's Tamworth home. Frances and Preston assisted Francis in the operation of the summer theater. She enjoyed the fact that virtually no one recognized the ticket seller as a former first lady, and the dignified Preston served as an usher. Frances commented that it gave her the opportunity to hear people's unguarded comments about the plays.[31] Francis and Alice had one daughter, Marion, who followed in her parents' footsteps and became an actress.

Photos taken of Frances as early as 1911 and 1912 show her with a pair of glasses suspended from a chain around her neck. As she aged, Frances developed additional problems with her eyesight. She wrote to her friend, Mrs. Thomas, in 1937,

> It was good to see your familiar writing on an envelope—and to read a letter from you—I'm sorry enough that such a necessity caused your letter—eyes are so important.
>
> I'm sorry too that I cannot give you the advice you ask—at once, but I am going to New York Friday, and I will send you an address as soon as I can leave there."[32]

Eight years later, Frances wrote her friend, "I have had cataracts removed from both eyes within the last eighteen months, and am now seeing better than I ever did, using both eyes. This was threatened for a long time, and we hoped it might not come in my life twice. But it hasn't been bad, and the reward is great."[33]

Frances had not let the diagnosis of blindness deter her. Facing the possibility, she taught herself Braille. When her sight was restored, she used her new skill to transcribe books for blind children.[34]

Whenever she received news coverage, reporters continued to write about her attractiveness and graciousness. One article said, "In conversation with Mrs. Preston, one has some difficulty remembering that she was the 'first lady' as far back as the 80's and 90's. Gracious in action and youthful in appearance, her personality and influence has been widely known and appreciated by 'younger generations' at Princeton University."[35]

In 1936, the San Francisco *Chronicle* wrote about her:

> The gracious and lovely woman who as Frances Folsom was a White House bride and as Mrs. Grover Cleveland was mistress of the mansion during her husband's two terms of office is in San Francisco this week—this time as a president in her own right.
>
> The former Mrs. Cleveland, now Mrs. Thomas Jex Preston, Jr., has for 11 years been national head of the

Needlework Guild of America and into this job of her own puts the love of humanity, the sympathy and loyalty that once was the aid and inspiration of one of America's great Presidents.[36]

A 1937 story on the surviving former first ladies characterized Frances this way: "Mrs. Preston, who as Mrs. Cleveland was called the most beautiful bride ever to enter the White House, is spending the Winter with her husband at Dunedin, Fla. Her grace and charm are as much in evidence today as when she presided over the social life of the nation's official mansion in those early days."[37]

Frances retained one perquisite of her years as first lady: the franking privilege. She was a conscientious and avid letter writer, and she kept her correspondence in a leather pouch. Her signature, "Frances F. Cleveland Preston," was clearly written in the upper-right-hand corner of the envelope in place of the stamp. Frances never accepted the $5,000 annual stipend that Congress eventually approved as a pension for presidential widows, but she took advantage of the free postage that was the last remaining vestige of her service to the country as the wife of a president.

Well into her seventies, Frances still attracted attention for her notable sense of fashion. The *Times* article noted: "While retaining a characteristic trait of never 'fussing' over her clothes, her taste is still cause for envy among her many friends. Well tailored, with browns and blues predominating, her wardrobe presents a distinguished rather than a chic appearance."[38]

Even in the last year of her life, Frances could still charm the people she met. Margaret Truman, daughter of President Harry Truman, met Frances in 1946, and described her as a "gracious and self-assured woman." Seated next to the former first lady at the bicentennial celebration of the founding of Princeton University, Truman discussed the renovations then under way at the White House. General Dwight Eisenhower was also seated at the table and, overhearing the conversation, he asked the woman who had been introduced as Mrs. Preston, "Where did you live in Washington?"

"The same place Margaret is living now," she [Frances] replied sweetly.

"Only then did I manage to inform Ike that he was talking to Mrs. Grover Cleveland," concluded Truman.[39]

In concluding her memoir, Jean Davis wrote: "The last time I saw Mrs. Preston I would not have known her had not my mother prompted me. I was not living in Princeton then and had not seen her for some years. The gracious manner was still there, but time had wrecked the physical loveliness. Today I put that later image out of my mind and turn back to the memory of the smiling lady in the carriage who held a frivolous little parasol in the fashionable pose of seventy years ago."[40]

# *Epilogue*

Frances traveled to Baltimore, Maryland, to celebrate the fiftieth birthday of her son Richard. She died in her sleep at his home, on October 29, 1947, a day before his birthday.

The obituaries recapped her life in brief, highlighting her White House wedding to Grover Cleveland, the births of her five children, and her marriage to Thomas Preston. Her four surviving children—Marion, Esther, Richard, and Francis—were named. No mention was made of her over fifty years of charity and philanthropic work, or of the efforts that she had extended to promote the cause of education for the very young and for women.

A private funeral service was held for her at the Presbyterian Church in Princeton, and she was interred at the Princeton Cemetery alongside Grover Cleveland and Ruth.

The memorial service held for her on November 9, in Tamworth, captured the essence of her life: a woman who was committed to duty, and who brought charm and beauty to every aspect of her life.

John Finley, Jr., aptly characterized Frances this way:

> My sister Ellen tells of asking her once whether she was not frightened when she first went to the White House, and of her answering that she was not frightened then, but was a little uneasy when she returned for the second term seven years later. "I suppose I knew more by that time," she said, one can almost see her smiling. Yet this story only tells once again, if there be need of re-telling of the miracle and the beauty of her utterly right instincts and of her perfect fidelity to them—traits which the most elaborate of training could not be sure of securing but which, lo, this young woman had and kept throughout her

life as naturally, seemingly, as the bird flies or the flower puts forth its bloom.

Yet to dwell on this perfection of intuition and instinct must not be to neglect the conscious and constant self-discipline which accompanied it. No one was more sympathetic and generous to others than she, nor more tolerant of them; yet she showed in a thousand ways how much she demanded of herself. Sometimes only a word suggested this hard self-schooling. "I will not let myself think that." Or again, it showed itself in long continued actions, as recently, when the danger arose that she might lose her sight, she steadily and patiently, yet almost gayly, taught herself Braille. And it was characteristic of her that even then she found someone else for whom she could work, and typed stories in Braille for a blind boy, who came to depend on her and for whom she continued to type even after the danger to her own sight had passed.

This serenity was also the profoundest and most beautiful of her traits. . . . As it rises above the heats and intensities of life, however much a person may have been involved in life, so it is in essence a deeply religious quality. It draws its strength from sources which the world hardly reckons with, and though a person may be remembered, as she is, for her grace, discipline and loving-kindness, yet even these noble and beautiful virtues are transcended at last by the quiet faith which is serenity of soul.[1]

# Afterword

When Frances Folsom married President Grover Cleveland, Rose Cleveland told the press, "My new sister is a woman capable of great development: a much stronger character than appears on the surface. She is a superior person."[1] History has proved Rose Cleveland correct.

From her first days in the White House, until her death over sixty years later, Frank conducted her life with a sense of purpose. She socialized with the most elite and influential members of American society in the late nineteenth century and early years of the twentieth century, while at the same time working tirelessly on behalf of the economic and educational needs of poor women and their children. Throughout her life, she was characterized as "gracious," "warm," and "caring." Colonel W. H. Crook and Ike Hoover, who were in her employ during her White House years, singled her out as one of the nation's kindest and most considerate first ladies.

Cleveland's second term generally places him in the category of "failed presidents," and Frances's reputation is coupled with his. That categorization, together with Frances's desire to stay out of the public eye, has caused many of her contributions to American life to fade from public view. She did, however, have a lasting impact on American education through her promotion of free kindergartens, her work to establish a college for women in New Jersey, and her tireless efforts as a trustee of her alma mater, Wells College, which is still educating students today.

Frances also had an effect on the office of first lady, as well. Betty Boyd Caroli wrote in her book, *First Ladies*, "What stands out most about Frances Cleveland, however, is the extent to which she underscores a change in style for First Ladies. Coming almost exactly forty years after Julia Tyler [until Frances, the nation's youngest first lady], Frances made no attempt to imitate the other woman's immaturity and almost childlike egotism. Rather than sitting on a raised platform to receive her guests in imitation of royalty as Julia Tyler had done, Frances was the model of simplicity and maturity, even though she was still in her twenties."[2]

In an interview with her hometown newspaper in 2001, Frances's granddaughter, Margaret Cleveland, commented: "I'd like to think that deep down inside her was an unconventional woman. Frances was not exactly a retiring wallflower."[3]

It is my hope that readers of this biography will agree with Ms. Cleveland.

# *Notes*

## CHAPTER 1

1. DeB. Randolph Keim, *Handbook of Official and Social Etiquette and Public Ceremonials at Washington*, 3rd ed. (Washington, DC: De B. Randolph Keim, 1889), 229.

2. "White House Bride," *New York Times*, 29 May 1886.

3. Ibid.

4. "The President's Wedding," *Washington Post*, 29 May 1886.

5. "White House Bride."

6. Ibid.

7. Ibid.

8. Allan Nevins, *Grover Cleveland: A Study in Courage* (Boston: Houghton Mifflin Co., 1933), 303.

9. "Played in the Orchard," *Boston Daily Globe*, 2 May 1886.

10. "Mrs. Grover Cleveland," *Atlanta Constitution*, 25 November 1888.

11. Katherine Willard, letter to Frances Folsom, 13 March 1886, Grover Cleveland Papers (GCP), Library of Congress.

12. Grover Cleveland to Mary Cleveland Hoyt, letter in Nevins, *Grover Cleveland*, 773–74.

13. Katherine Willard, letter to Frances Folsom, 18 February 1886, GCP.

14. Nevins, *Grover Cleveland*, 303.

15. "The President's Wedding," *New York Times*, 26 May 1886.

16. "Miss Folsom's Return," *New York Times*, 27 May 1886.

17. "Colonel Lamont's Mission," *New York Times*, 27 May 1886.

18. Nevins, *Grover Cleveland*, 773–74.

19. "Cleveland and His Bride," *New York Times*, 31 May 1886.

20. Ibid.

21. "The Nation's First Lady," *New York Times*, 3 June 1886.

22. Ibid.

23. Stephen Gwynn, *The Letters and Friendships of Sir Cecil Spring-Rice, A Record*, vol. 1 (Boston: Houghton Mifflin Co., 1929), 63.

24. Patricia O'Toole, *The Five of Hearts* (New York: Simon & Schuster, 1990), 149.

25. "Married!" *Washington Post*, 3 June 1886.

26. Ibid.

27. Ibid.

## CHAPTER 2

1. "A Terrible Accident," *Buffalo Daily Courier*, 24 July 1875.

2. Ibid.

3. "Mrs. Cleveland's Father," *Boston Daily Globe*, 28 June 1886.

4. Ibid.

5. Handwritten recollection of Susan Cleveland Yeomans, 1908, Grover Cleveland Papers (GCP), section 9, Library of Congress.

6. Chauncey M. Depew, *My Memories of Eighty Years* (New York: Charles Scribner's Sons, 1922), 124.

7. Oscar Folsom, letter to Emma Cornelia Harmon, 30 November 1862, Grover Cleveland Papers (GCP), Library of Congress. This was enclosed with a letter from Frank's mother to her that read: "I am reading over, and destroying, your dear Papa's letters, written before we were married because I am so much alone I know not into whose hands they might fall, and they are very sacred to me. I send you a part of one—how curiously things have come about" (January 23, 1896). A request in Frank's handwriting, along the margin of her father's letter, "Please destroy," was obviously not followed.

8. "Miss Folsom's History," *New York Times*, 31 May 1886.

9. Jane Marsh Dieckmann, *Wells College: A History* (Aurora, NY: Wells College Press. 1995), 1.

10. Ibid., 6.

11. Ibid., 62.

12. Ibid.

13. Jean S. Davis, "A Rambling Memoir of Mrs. Grover Cleveland and Some Related History" (unpublished manuscript, Louis Jefferson Long Library, Wells College, Aurora, NY, n.d.), 1.

14. *Wells College*, 62.

15. "They All Loved Her," *Cleveland Leader*, January (n.d.) 1894.

16. Nevins, *Grover Cleveland*, 302.

17. "They All Loved Her."

18. "Mrs. Cleveland at Wells," *New York World*, 8 November 1892.

19. W. J. Lampton, "Mrs. Cleveland as a College Girl," *Ladies' Home Journal*, March 1904, 12.

20. Donna Folsom Wollitz, "The Frances Folsom Cleveland Story," (Princeton Historical Society, Princeton, NJ, 10 August 1990), 9.

21. Ibid.


CHAPTER 3


1. "Mountain Honeymoon," *New York Times*, 4 June 1886.

2. Grover Cleveland, letter to Daniel S. Lamont, 3 June 1886, quoted in Allan Nevins, *Letters of Grover Cleveland, 1850–1908* (Boston: Houghton Mifflin Co., 1933), 112–13.

3. "A Tremendous Undertaking," from the *Chicago Tribune*, quoted in the *Washington Post*, 6 June 1886.

4. Ibid.

5. "In Honor of the Bride," *New York Times*, 7 June 1886.

6. Ibid.

7. Frank G. Carpenter, *Carp's Washington* (New York: McGraw-Hill Book Co., 1960), 1, 3.

8. Jean Strouse, *Morgan: American Financier* (New York: Random House 1999), 287.

9. Stephen Gwynn, *The Letters and Friendships of Sir Cecil Spring-Rice, A Record*, vol. 1 (Boston: Houghton Mifflin Co., 1929), 63.

10. "A Welcome to the Bride," *Washington Post*, 16 June 1886.

11. Frances F. Cleveland, note to Daniel Lamont, 1 July 1886, Grover Cleveland Papers (GCP), Library of Congress. The actual days of the receptions were Tuesdays and Thursdays.

12. Colonel W. H. Crook, *Memories of the White House* (Boston: Little, Brown and Company, 1911), 185, retrieved from http:books.google.com.

13. "Society," *Washington Post*, 11 July 1886, 9.

14. Crook, *Memories of the White House*, 184.

15. "Pleasures at Deer Park," *Washington Post*, 6 June 1886.

16. Crook, 185–86.

17. "Homage of the People," *Washington Post*, 19 June 1886.

18. "Mrs. Cleveland at Home," *Washington Post*, 26 June 1886.

19. Grover Cleveland, letter to S. B. Ward, 8 August 1886, quoted in Nevins, *Letters of Grover Cleveland*, 117.

20. Grover Cleveland, letter to Daniel S. Lamont, 3 June 1886, quoted in Nevins, *Letters of Grover Cleveland*, 112–13.

21. Quoted in "Not Without her Husband," *New York Times*, 7 September 1887.

22. Grover Cleveland, letter to George J. Hepmouth, 9 September 1887, quoted in Nevins, *Letters of Grover Cleveland*, 151.

23. Allan Nevins, *Grover Cleveland: A Study in Courage* (Boston: Houghton Mifflin Co., 1933), 310.

24. Grover Cleveland, "Would Woman Suffrage Be Unwise?" *Ladies' Home Journal*, October 1905, 7.

## CHAPTER 4

1. Mrs. W. B. Hayward, letter to Frances F. Cleveland, 28 March 1887, Grover Cleveland Papers (GCP), Library of Congress.

2. Mrs. M. J. Muldoon, letter to Frances F. Cleveland, 29 June 1887, GCP. The writer misspelled the name of Cleveland's Postmaster General, Vilas.

3. Mattie H. Cain, letter to Frances F. Cleveland, 20 September 1887, GCP.

4. Ada Elsemore, letter to Frances F. Cleveland, 20 September 1887, GCP.

5. Julia Millikin Severance, "Diary" (unpublished copy), entry for 23 November 1887 (Louis Jefferson Long Library, Wells College, Aurora, NY).

6. Allan Nevins, *Grover Cleveland: A Study in Courage* (Boston: Houghton Mifflin Co., 1933), 312.

7. Stephen Gwynn, *The Letters and Friendships of Sir Cecil Spring-Rice, A Record*, vol. 1 (Boston: Houghton Mifflin Co., 1929), 72.

8. Ibid., 72–73.

9. Richard Watson Gilder, letter to Frances F. Cleveland, 29 June 1887, GCP.

10. Ibid.

11. Frances F. Cleveland, letter to Richard Watson Gilder, 29 June 1887, Lilly Library (LL), Indiana University.

12. Grover Cleveland to Leo Oppenheim, quoted in Allan Nevins, *Letters of Grover Cleveland, 1850–1908* (Boston: Houghton Mifflin Co., 1933), 321.

13. Frances F. Cleveland, letter to Richard Watson Gilder, 29 June 1887, LL.

14. Richard Watson Gilder, letter to Frances F. Cleveland, 29 June 1887, GCP.

15. Frances F. Cleveland, letter to Helena Gilder, 9 October 1887, LL.

16. Frances F. Cleveland, letter to Helena Gilder, 16 October 1887, LL.

17. Frances F. Cleveland, letter to Richard and Helena Gilder, 24 October 1887, LL.

18. Severance, "Diary," entry for 23 November 1887.

19. Ibid.

20. Ibid.

21. Severance, "Diary," 24 November 1887.

22. Frances F. Cleveland, letter to Helena Gilder, 28 November 1887, LL.

23. Frances F. Cleveland, letter to Helena Gilder, 15 December 1887, LL.

24. Ibid.

## CHAPTER 5

1. "Mrs. Grover Cleveland at Home," *New York Times*, 25 December 1887.

2. Frank G. Carpenter, *Carp's Washington* (New York: McGraw-Hill Book Co., 1960), 47.

3. "Frances Cleveland Clubs," *Atlanta Constitution*, 6 March 1888.

4. Grover Cleveland, "Woman's Mission and Woman's Clubs," *Ladies' Home Journal*, May 1905, 4.

5. Grover Cleveland to Mrs. Mary Frost Ormsby, quoted in Allan Nevins, *Letters of Grover Cleveland, 1850–1908* (Boston: Houghton Mifflin Co., 1933), 291.

6. "National Capital Topics," *New York Times*, 18 March 1888.

7. Frances F. Cleveland, letter to Richard Watson Gilder, 12 November 1887, Lilly Library (LL), Indiana University.

8. "Why Greeley Favored Fremont," *New York Times*, 14 June 1888.

9. Stephen Gwynn, *The Letters and Friendships of Sir Cecil Spring-Rice, A Record*, vol. 1 (Boston: Houghton Mifflin Co., 1929), 91.

10. "No White House Scandal," *Chicago Tribune*, 7 December 1888.

11. Ibid.

12. "An Early Campaign Slander," *New York Times*, 5 June 1888.

13. "The Stories about the President," *New York Times*, 10 June 1888.

14. Frances F. Cleveland, letter to Mrs. Maggie Nicodemus, 3 June 1888, Grover Cleveland Papers (GCP), Library of Congress.

15. Note written on letter of Frances F. Cleveland to Mrs. Maggie Nicodemus, 3 June 1888, GCP.

16. "Mrs. Cleveland's Answer," *New York Times*, 7 June 1888.

17. "Slandered Jefferson, Too," *New York Times*, 10 June 1888.

18. "A Merry Coaching Party," *New York Times*, 29 May 1888.

19. "Receiving Mrs. Cleveland," *New York Times*, 27 May 1888.

20. Letter from Frances F. Cleveland to Allan Marquand, quoted in "The First Lady Lunched at Guernsey Hall," *Princeton Recollector*, Summer 1978, 9.

21. "Mrs. Grover Cleveland at Marion," *New York Times*, 28 July 1888.

22. "A Chapter on the Bustle," *Atlanta Constitution*, 7 November 1892.

23. Ibid.

24. http://www.archives.gov/federal-register/electoral-college/scores.html#1888.

25. "The White House Ladies," *Atlanta Constitution*, 10 November 1888.

26. "Mrs. Grover Cleveland," *Atlanta Constitution*, 25 November 1888.

27. "To Help Wells College," *New York Times*, 16 November 1888.

28. "Mrs. Grover Cleveland."

29. Ibid.

30. "National Capital Topics," *New York Times*, 18 March 1888.

31. "White House Ladies."

32. Colonel W. H. Crook, *Memories of the White House* (Boston: Little, Brown and Company, 1911), 198, retrieved from http:books.google.com.

CHAPTER 6

1. Katherine Willard, letter to Frances F. Cleveland, 10 March 1889, Grover Cleveland Papers (GCP), Library of Congress.

2. Minnie Alexander, letter to Frances F. Cleveland, 24 March 1889, GCP.

3. Frances F. Cleveland, letter to Richard Watson Gilder, 12 November 1887, Lilly Library (LL), Indiana University.

4. Grover Cleveland, letter to William F. Vilas, 20 May 1889, quoted in Allan Nevins, *Letters of Grover Cleveland, 1850–1908* (Boston: Houghton Mifflin Co., 1933), 207.

5. Emma Folsom Perrine, letter to Frances F. Cleveland, 1 July 1889, GCP.

6. Ibid.

7. Frances F. Cleveland, letter to Mrs. R. Townsend, 26 May 1889, GCP.

8. Mrs. R. Townsend, letter to Frances F. Cleveland, 31 May 1889, GCP.

9. "Plan of the Clevelands," *Chicago Tribune*, 1 December 1889.

10. "Mrs. Cleveland's Hopes," *New York Times*, 4 March 1889, 5.

11. "The Exhibition Opened," *New York Times*, 18 April 1889, 1.

12. Frances F. Cleveland, letter to Helena Gilder, 18 May 1889, LL.

13. Grover Cleveland, letter to Frances F. Cleveland, 5 June 1889, GCP.

14. Grover Cleveland, letter to Frances F. Cleveland, 12 June 1889, GCP.

15. Grover Cleveland, letter to Frances F. Cleveland, 18 June 1889, 20 June 1889, GCP.

16. Minnie Alexander, letter to Frances F. Cleveland, 22 June 1889, GCP.

17. Katherine Willard, letter to Frances F. Cleveland, 28 August 1889, GCP.

18. Katherine Willard, letter to Frances F. Cleveland, 4 September 1889, GCP.

19. Arthur John, *The Best Years of the Century: Richard Watson Gilder, "Scribner's Monthly," and the "Century Magazine," 1870–1909* (Urbana: University of Illinois Press, 1981), 2.

20. Frances F. Cleveland, letter to Richard Watson Gilder, 8 July 1889.

21. Richard Watson Gilder, poem to Frances F. Cleveland, undated, GCP.

22. Ibid.

23. Elizabeth Dale Ross, *The Kindergarten Crusade* (Athens: Ohio University Press, 1976), 19.

24. "What Kindergartens Do," *New York Times*, 17 March 1895.

25. "New York and the Kindergarten," *Critic* 17, no. 14 (December 1890): 313–14.

26. "Visited by Mrs. Cleveland," *New York Times*, 13 November 1892.

27. "Melody, Joy and Charity," *New York Times*, 25 December 1890.

28. "Pennsylvania Deer Hunting," *New York Times*, 23 December 1890.

29. "Invited by Mr. Cleveland," *New York Times*, 22 May 1890; "Mrs. Cleveland a Flower Girl," *New York Times*, 23 May 1890.

30. "Society Topics of the Week," *New York Times*, 12 April 1891.

31. Frances F. Cleveland, letter to Helena Gilder, 27 September 1890, LL.

32. Frances F. Cleveland, letter to Helena Gilder, 22 May 1891, LL.

33. Frances F. Cleveland, letter to Helena Gilder, 30 September 1891, LL.

34. Grover Cleveland, letter to Wilson S. Bissell, 21 October 1891, quoted in Nevins, *Letters of Grover Cleveland*, 269.

35. Emma Folsom Perrine, letter to Helena Gilder, 5 October 1891, LL.

36. Frances F. Cleveland, letter to Helena Gilder, 6 December 1891, LL.

37. Ibid.

38. Frances F. Cleveland, letter to Richard Watson Gilder, 16 December 1891, LL.

39. Frances F. Cleveland, letter to Helena Gilder, 21 December 1891, LL.

## CHAPTER 7

1. Frances F. Cleveland, letter to Helena Gilder, 30 November 1892, Lilly Library (LL), Indiana University.

2. "Society Topics of the Week," *New York Times*, 13 November 1892.

3. Frances F. Cleveland, letter to Helena Gilder, 30 November 1892, LL.

4. Edward J. Stellwagen, letter to Mr. Wilson, 23 March 1893, Grover Cleveland Papers (GCP), Library of Congress.

5. "Cabinet Officers' Wives," *New York Times*, 26 February 1893.

6. "Happenings of the Day," *New York Times*, 5 March 1893.

7. Irwin (Ike) Hoover, "Mrs. Cleveland Weeps," *Saturday Evening Post*, 10 March 1934, 16.

8. Ibid.

9. Hilary A. Herbert, "Grover Cleveland and His Cabinet at Work," *Century*, March 1913, 744.

10. Memoranda, n.d., GCP.

11. "Gossip of Social Circles," *Washington Post*, 18 March 1893.

12. Emma Folsom Perrine, letter to Frances F. Cleveland, 23 March 1893, GCP.

13. Ibid.

14. In the second Cleveland administration, Frances eliminated her Saturday receptions and received the public on Tuesdays and Fridays. Katherine Willard, letter to Frances F. Cleveland, 23 April 1893, GCP.

15. Helen Fairchild Smith, letter to Frances F. Cleveland, 28 March 1893, GCP.

16. J. I. Connor, letter to Frances F. Cleveland, 17 May 1893, GCP.

17. Frances F. Cleveland, letter to Helena Gilder, 7 May 1893, GCP.

18. "The President's Reception," *Washington Post*, 20 May 1893.

19. "Prince Antoine on the Box," *Washington Post*, 24 May 1893.

20. Wilbur Cross and John Moses, "My God, sir, I think the President is doomed," *American History Illustrated*, November 1982, 41.

21. Ibid., 41–42.

22. Ibid., 41.

23. "Will Go to Buzzard's Bay," *Washington Post*, 11 June 1893.

24. "The President's Vacation," *New York Times*, 20 June 1893.

25. "To Their Seaside Cottage," *Washington Post*, 19 June 1893.

26. "The President's Vacation," *New York Times*, 20 June 1893.

27. "Off for Buzzard's Bay," *Washington Post*, 21 June 1893.

28. William Williams Keen, MD, "The President's Operation," *Saturday Evening Post*, 22 September, 1917, 106, 108.

29. Ibid.

30. Ibid.

31. "No Sight of the President," *Washington Post*, 5 July 1893.

32. "Thinking of Fishing," *Boston Daily Globe*, 8 July 1893.

33. Ibid.

34. Ibid.

35. Keen, MD, 108.

36. "Thinking of Fishing."

37. Ibid.

38. "Back at Buzzard's Bay," *Washington Post*, 20 July 1893.

39. Frances F. Cleveland, letter to Joseph Jefferson, quoted in Robert McNutt McElroy, *Grover Cleveland, the Man and the Statesman; An Authorized Biography*, vol. 2 (New York: Harper Brothers, 1923), 29.

40. Frances F. Cleveland, letter to William E. Russell, 31 July 1893, quoted in Allan Nevins, *The Letters of Grover Cleveland, 1850–1908* (Boston: Houghton Mifflin Co., 1933), 329.

41. Emma Folsom Perrine, letter to Frances F. Cleveland, 24 July 1893, GCP.

42. Richard Olney, "From Memorandum by Richard Olney," GCP, series 9, subseries A, undated.
43. Frances F. Cleveland, letter to Helena and Richard Gilder, 27 July 1893, LL.
44. "Back at Buzzard's Bay," *Washington Post*, 20 July 1893, 1.
45. Cross and Moses, "My God, sir," 45.
46. "Born at the White House," *Washington Post*, 10 September 1893.
47. Kate Douglas Wiggins, letter to Frances F. Cleveland, 10 September 1893.
48. Grover Cleveland, letter to Mrs. John G. Carlisle, 14 September 1893, quoted in Nevins, *Letters of Grover Cleveland*, 335.
49. "Momentous Day," *Boston Daily Globe*, 10 September 1893.
50. "The President and His Family," *Washington Post*, 18 November 1893.
51. Irwin (Ike) Hood Hoover, *Forty-two Years in the White House* (Boston: Houghton Mifflin Co., 1934), 13.
52. Frances F. Cleveland, letter to Helena Gilder, 15 December 1893, LL.
53. "The Social Calendar," *Washington Post*, 17 December 1893.
54. "White House Smiles," *Washington Post*, 24 December 1893.
55. Irwin (Ike) Hoover, "Mrs. Cleveland Weeps," *Saturday Evening Post*, 10 March 1934, 17.
56. Colonel W. H. Crook, *Memories of the White House* (Boston: Little, Brown and Company, 1911), 192, retrieved from http:books.google.com.
57. Jean S. Davis, "A Rambling Memoir of Mrs. Grover Cleveland and Some Related History" (unpublished manuscript, Louis Jefferson Long Library, Wells College, Aurora, NY, n.d.), 7–8.

## CHAPTER 8

1. "Plans of the Polite," *Washington Post*, 24 December 1893.
2. "Mrs. Cleveland's Reception," *New York Times*, 21 January 1894.
3. Frances F. Cleveland, letter to Helena Gilder, 14 April 1894, Lilly Library (LL), Indiana University.
4. Frances F. Cleveland, letter to Helena Gilder, 3 June 1894, LL.
5. Irwin (Ike) Hood Hoover, *Forty Years in the White House* (Boston: Houghton Mifflin Co., 1934), 15.

6. Barbara S. Rivette, *Grover Cleveland: Fayetteville's Hometown Boy* (New York: Fayetteville-Manlius School District, Instructional Communications Center, 1987), 14.

7. Frances F. Cleveland, letter to Helena Gilder, 11 November 1894, LL.

8. Frances F. Cleveland, letter to Helena Gilder, 18 November 1894, LL.

9. "Under Society Favor," *Washington Post*, 28 February 1894.

10. "Pensoara Kindergarten Benefit," *Washington Post*, 5 December 1894.

11. "To Teach the President's Daughters," *New York Times*, 6 September 1896.

12. "The Congress of Mothers," *New York Times*, 18 February 1897.

13. "Her Charities," *Atlanta*, 2 April 1893.

14. Irwin (Ike) Hood Hoover, "Mrs. Cleveland Weeps," *Saturday Evening Post*, 10 March 1934.

15. "Women Must Make a Choice," *New York Times*, 28 January 1894.

16. Ibid.

17. Frances F. Cleveland, letter to Helena Gilder, 16 June 1895, LL.

18. Emma Folsom Perrine, letter to Helena Gilder, 11 July 1895, LL.

19. Frances F. Cleveland, letter to Helena and Richard Gilder, 22 July 1895, LL.

20. Frances F. Cleveland Preston, interview with Allan Nevins, quoted in Allan Nevin, *Grover Cleveland: A Study in Courage* (Boston: Houghton Mifflin Co., 1933), 726.

21. Hoover, "Mrs. Cleveland Weeps," 46.

22. Ibid.

23. Ibid.

24. Ibid.

CHAPTER 9

1. Jean S. Davis, "A Rambling Memoir of Mrs. Grover Cleveland and Some Related History" (unpublished manuscript, Louis Jefferson Long Library, Wells College, Aurora, NY, n.d.), 8.

2. Ibid., 13.

3. Allan Nevins, *Grover Cleveland: A Study in Courage* (Boston: Houghton Mifflin Co., 1933), 731–32.

4. Frances F. Cleveland, letter to Richard and Helena Gilder, 2 November 1897, Lilly Library (LL), Indiana University.

5. Frances F. Cleveland, letter to Richard and Helena Gilder, 27 December 1897, LL.

6. Frances F. Cleveland, letter to Richard and Helena Gilder, 3 March 1898, LL.

7. Eleanor Wilson McAdoo, *The Woodrow Wilsons* (New York: Macmillan, 1937), 56.

8. Frances F. Cleveland, letter to Theodore Roosevelt, 26 June 1902, Theodore Roosevelt Papers (TRP), series 1, Library of Congress.

9. Frances F. Cleveland, letter to Theodore Roosevelt, 12 July 1902, TRP.

10. "Death List of a Day," *New York Times*, 1 June 1901.

11. Frances F. Cleveland, letter to Martha Waller Johnson, 2 January 1902, Martha Waller Johnson Papers (MWJP), Virginia Historical Society.

12. Ibid.

13. Frances F. Cleveland, letter to Martha Waller Johnson, 23 March 1903, MWJP.

14. Frances F. Cleveland, letter to Helena and Richard Gilder, 12 January 1904, LL.

15. Martha Finley, letter to Helena Gilder, 15 January 1904, LL.

16. "Son Keeps President's Name on Stage," *Chicago Tribune*, 28 June 1984.

17. Frances F. Cleveland, letter to Martha Waller Johnson, 17 December 1907, MWJP.

18. Frances F. Cleveland, letter to Martha Waller Johnson, 4 March 1908, MWJP.

19. Frances F. Cleveland, letter to Helena Gilder, 10 April 1908, LL.

20. Frances F. Cleveland, letter to Helena Gilder, 30 April 1908, LL.

21. Frances F. Cleveland, telegram to Richard W. Gilder, 24 June 1908, GCP.

22. Richard Watson Gilder, *A Record of Friendship* (New York: The Century Company, 1910), 458.

23. Ibid., 459.

24. Ibid., 460.

25. "The Funeral Ceremonies at Princeton," *Harper's Weekly*, 4 July 1908, 7.

26. "Died Poor, Say His Friends," *New York Times*, 25 June 1908.

27. Various tax receipts, GCP, series 3.

28. Handwritten account of stock ownership, GCP, series 3.

29. Andrew Carnegie, telegram to Frank S. Hastings, 29 September 1908, courtesy Grover Cleveland Birthplace Museum, Caldwell, NJ.

30. "Grover Cleveland on the Campaign and His Prophecy of the Result," *New York Times*, 30 August 1908.

31. "Signature Not Her Husband's," *Boston Daily Globe*, 16 June 1909.

32. Frances F. Cleveland, letter to Andrew Carnegie, 28 September 1908, courtesy Grover Cleveland Birthplace Museum.

33. Ibid.

34. "He Fails to Face Larceny Charge," *Atlanta Constitution*, 2 February 1909.

35. "Signature Not Her Husband's."

36. Memoranda and letters, GCP.

37. "National Leaders Eulogize Cleveland," *New York Times*, 19 March 1909.

38. Frances F. Cleveland, letter to Richard Watson Gilder, 23 March 1909.

39. Frances F. Cleveland, letter to Helena Gilder, 2 March 1909, LL.

40. Frances F. Cleveland, letter to Martha Waller Johnson, 13 September 1909, WP.


CHAPTER 10


1. Frances F. Cleveland, letter to Helena Gilder, 12 November 1909, Lilly Library (LL), Indiana University.

2. Ibid.

3. Frances F. Cleveland, letter to Helena Gilder, 21 November 1909, LL.

4. "Mrs. Cleveland and Children," *Atlanta Constitution*, 30 May 1910.

5. Jean S. Davis, "A Rambling Memoir of Mrs. Grover Cleveland and Some Related History" (unpublished manuscript, Louis Jefferson Long Library, Wells College, Aurora, NY, n.d.), 14.

6. Ibid.

7. Jane Marsh Dieckmann, *Wells College: A History* (Aurora, NY: Wells College Press, 1995) 99.

8. Ibid., 96.

9. Ibid., 98.

10. Ibid.

11. Davis, "Rambling Memoir," 16.

12. Dieckmann, *Wells College,* 99.

13. Davis, "Rambling Memoir," 21–22.

14. "Mrs. Cleveland to Marry Again," *New York Times,* 30 October 1912.

15. "Mrs. Cleveland's Fiancé is Modest and Camera Shy," *Auburn Citizen,* undated.

16. Frances F. Cleveland, telegram to Helena Gilder, 31 October 1912, LL.

17. Frances F. Cleveland, letter to Helena Gilder, 1 November 1912, LL.

18. "Princeton Won't Let Mrs. Cleveland Go," *New York Times,* 1 November 1912.

19. "Beckons Mrs. Cleveland," *New York Times,* 1 November 1912.

20. Davis, "Rambling Memoir," 23.

21. Irwin (Ike) Hood Hoover, *Forty-two Years in the White House* (Boston: Houghton Mifflin Co., 1934), 46–47.

22. "Mrs. Cleveland and Prof. Preston Wed.," *New York Times,* 11 February 1913.

23. Frances F. Cleveland Preston, letter to Helena Gilder, 9 February 1913, LL.

24. Davis, "Rambling Memoir," 24.

25. News clipping, unknown source, 1940, provided courtesy Grover Cleveland Birthplace Museum.

26. Isabel F. Harmon, "Memoir," ix.

27. Naomi Getsoyan Topalian, *Legacy of Honor* (Watertown, MA: Baikar Publications, 1995), 275.

28. Davis, "Rambling Memoir," 23.

29. Frances F. Cleveland Preston, letter to Helena Gilder, 9 March 1913, LL.

30. "Old Cleveland Home Is Taken for Nation," *New York Times,* 19 March 1913.

31. "Mrs. Preston Joins Antis," *New York Times,* 2 May 1913.

32. "Reasons Why the Women of New Jersey Oppose Equal Suffrage," New Jersey Historical Society. Amelia Berndt Moorfield Collection. Available from: http://www.scc.rutgers.edu/njwomenhistory/Period_4/antisuffrageb.htm.

33. "Mrs. Preston Is on Second Trip to This Section," *Asheville Citizen,* 5 May 1932.

34. Sue Severn, "Frances Folsom Cleveland," in *American First Ladies: Their Lives and Legacy*, ed. Lewis Gould (New York: Garland Publishing, 1996), 258.

35. "Son Keeps President's Name on Stage," *Chicago Tribune*, 28 June 1984.

## CHAPTER 11

1. Frances F. Cleveland Preston, letter to Helena Gilder, 16 March 1914, Lilly Library (LL), Indiana University.

2. John Carver Edwards, *Patriots in Pinstripe* (Washington, DC: University Press of America, 1982), 1. *Patriots in Pinstripe*, which may well be the only existing comprehensive history of the National Security League, described Preston as "Professor Thomas J. Preston, Jr., an archaeologist from Wells College in Aurora, New York." The book's source for the description of Preston was a publication of the National Security League entitled, *The Flying Squadron of Speakers: A Propaganda Regiment for Patriotic Service*. There is no mention of Preston's marriage to the widow of the late President Cleveland, and there is also no reference to Preston's one-year tenure in his position as secretary of the Speakers' Bureau, or that his wife later replaced him in the position.

3. Frances F. Cleveland Preston, letter to Helena Gilder, 8 July 1914, Lilly Library (LL), Indiana University.

4. Frank S. Hastings, letter to Mrs. Daniel S. Lamont, 31 August 1914, Grover Cleveland Papers (GCP), Library of Congress.

5. Frank S. Hastings, letter to unnamed recipients, 3 September 1914, GCP.

6. Frank S. Hastings, letter to unnamed recipients, no day given, September 1914, GCP.

7. "Refugees from Genoa," *Boston Globe*, 2 October 1914.

8. Frances F. Cleveland Preston, letter to Helena Gilder, 5 October 1914, LL.

9. "Would Shoot All Spies," *New York Times*, 4 March 1918.

10. Edwards, *Patriots in Pinstripe*, 4.

11. Ibid., 91.

12. Ibid., 7, 9.

13. Theodore Roosevelt, letter to Mrs. Frances F. Cleveland Preston, Theodore Roosevelt Papers (TRP), Library of Congress.

14. "Former Mrs. Cleveland Teaches Patriotism," *New York Times*, 27 January 1918.

15. "Mrs. Preston Bureau Head," *New York Times*, 3 November 1918.

16. Edwards, *Patriots in Pinstripe*, 101.

17. Kathleen Burke, telegram to Theodore Roosevelt with copy to Mrs. Preston, National Security League, 23 May 1918, TRP.

18. Frances F. Cleveland Preston, letter to Theodore Roosevelt, 23 May 1918, TRP.

19. Edwards, *Patriots in Pinstripe*, 115.

20. Frances F. Cleveland Preston, letter to Theodore Roosevelt, 25 June 1918, TRP.

21. Edwards, *Patriots in Pinstripe*, 115–16.

22. "Pack Carnegie Hall for War Aid Rally," *New York Times*, 18 October 1917.

23. "Urges Women to Unite," *New York Times*, 29 April 1918.

24. Robert D. Ward, "The Origin and Activities of the National Security League: 1914–1919," *Mississippi Valley Historical Review* 47, no. 1 (June 1960): 64.

25. Ibid., 64–65.

26. "Esther Cleveland Weds Capt. Bosanquet," *New York Times*, 15 March 1918.

27. "Marion Cleveland, Bride in Princeton," *New York Times*, 29 November 1917.

28. Frances F. Cleveland Preston, letter to Theodore Roosevelt, 25 June 1918, TRP.

29. "Women in Campaign for Permanent Peace," *New York Times*, 21 January 1918.

30. "Taft Warns Nation Against Peace Trap," *New York Times*, 22 February 18.

31. "Women Ask Ban on Beer," *New York Times*, 1 March 1918.

32. "Decries Women Delegates," *New York Times*, 17 November 1918.

## CHAPTER 12

1. "Mortuary," *Atlanta Constitution*, 28 December 1915.

2. Frances F. Cleveland Preston, letter to Helena Gilder, 23 January 1916, Lilly Library (LL), Indiana University.

3. "R. W. Gilder's Widow Dies," *New York Times*, 29 May 1916.

4. Frances F. Cleveland Preston, letter to Robert McElroy, 28 December 1919, Grover Cleveland Papers (GCP), series 3, Library of Congress.

5. William Gorham Rice, letter to Frances F. Cleveland Preston, 15 August 1919, GCP, series 3.

6. "Cleveland Extolled at Natal Day Service," *New York Times*, 14 March 1932.

7. Frances F. Cleveland Preston, letter to Mrs. Henry F. Vilas, 20 June 1922, GCP, series 3.

8. Margaret Bissell Dell, letter to Frances F. Cleveland Preston, June 1922, GCP, series 3.

9. Frances F. Cleveland Preston, letter to James F. Tracey, June 1922, GCP, series 3.

10. L. R. McCabe, "Work of the Guild," *Harper's Bazaar*, 23 December 1899, 1116.

11. Charles Albert Selden, "Six White House Wives and Widows," *Ladies' Home Journal*, June 1927, 19.

12. "Mrs. Preston's New Work," *New York Times*, 24 December 1925.

13. Margaret Hickey, "A Lift of Heart for Helper and Helped," *Ladies' Home Journal*, December 1959, 17.

14. "Younger Campers to Hear Grenfell," *New York Times*, 7 August 1933.

15. "Mrs. Preston Is on Second Trip to This Section," *Asheville Citizen*, 5 May 1932.

16. Ibid.

17. Ibid.

18. "Heads Needlework Guild," *New York Times*, 5 May 1939.

19. Jean S. Davis, "A Rambling Memoir of Mrs. Grover Cleveland and Some Related History," (unpublished manuscript, Louis Jefferson Long Library, Wells College, Aurora, NY, n.d., 28). Jane Marsh Dieckmann, *Wells College: A History* (Aurora, NY: Wells College Press, 1995), 116..

20. Frances F. Cleveland Preston, letter to Mrs. M. S. Thomas, 8 October 1920, GCP, series 3.

21. Ibid.

22. Frances F. Cleveland Preston, letter to Mrs. M. S. Thomas, 19 October 1920, GCP, series 3.

23. Frances F. Cleveland Preston, letter to Mrs. M. S. Thomas, 28 February 1921, GCP, series 3.

24. Frances F. Cleveland Preston, letter to Mrs. M. S. Thomas, 8 November 1922, GCP, series 3.

25. Frances F. Cleveland Preston, letter to Mrs. M. S. Thomas, 30 December 1922, GCP, series 3.

26. Frances F. Cleveland Preston, letter to Mrs. M. S. Thomas, 7 May 1923, GCP, series 3.

27. "Marion Cleveland, Bride in Princeton," *New York Times*, 29 November 1917.

28. "Mrs. William S. Dell Gains Paris Divorce," *New York Times*, 17 February 1926.

29. "Pedigree of: Stephen Grover Cleveland 1937–1908"; available from: http://www.concentric.net/~pvb/GEN/presclev.html.

30. "Cleveland Wedding Plans," *New York Times*, 17 May 1925.

31. Sue Severn, "Frances Folsom Cleveland," in *American First Ladies: Their Lives and Legacy*, ed. Lewis Gould (New York: Garland Publishing, 1996), 258.

32. Frances F. Cleveland Preston, to Mrs. M. S. Thomas, 16 June 1937, GCP, series 3.

33. Frances F. Cleveland Preston, to Mrs. M. S. Thomas, 28 March 1945, GCP, series 3.

34. Ibid.

35. "Mrs. Preston Is on Second Trip to This Section."

36. "Mrs. Preston Needlework Guild Head," *San Francisco Chronicle*, 22 May 1936.

37. "First Ladies of Other Years Are Still Ruled by Reticence," *New York Times*, 7 February 1937.

38. Ibid.

39. Margaret Truman, *First Ladies* (New York: Random House, 1995), 345.

40. Davis, "Rambling Memoir," 29.

EPILOGUE

1. John H. Finley, Jr., "Memorial Service for Mrs. Preston at the Congregational Church," Tamworth, New Hampshire, 9 November 1947.

AFTERWORD

1. "Miss Cleveland's Opinion," *Philadelphia Press*, quoted in the *Washington Post*, 6 June 1886.

2. Betty Boyd Caroli, *First Ladies* (New York: Oxford University Press, 1987), 106.

3. "First Lady Cleveland: The View from Inside," *Portland Press Herald*, 18 January 2001.

# *Bibliography*

## BOOKS AND WEB SITES

Adams, Ellen E. " 'Of more consequence than the president': Frances Folsom Cleveland and the Role of First Lady in the Nineteenth Century." MA thesis, College of William and Mary, 2004.

"American President.org." <http://www.americanpresident.org/history/grover-cleveland/firstlady/>.

"Barnstormers History." <http://barnstomerstheater.com/barnstomers_history.htm>.

Blackwell, Jon. "1908: Gruff Old Grover." <http://www.capitalcentury.com/1908.html>.

Bordin, Ruth. *Frances Willard*. Chapel Hill: University of North Carolina Press, 1986.

Brodsky, Alyn. *Grover Cleveland: A Study in Character*. New York: St. Martin's Press, 2001.

Buffalo City Directory. <http://distantcousin.com/Directories/NY/Buffalo/1869/Image/254.jpg>.

Buffalonian. "The Buffalo Guard—Western New York History." <http://www.buffalonian.com/history/industry/military/militiahofniagaraV1p452.html>.

Carnegie, Andrew. *The Autobiography of Andrew Carnegie*. Boston:Houghton Mifflin Co., 1920.

Carpenter, Frank G. *Carp's Washington*. New York. McGraw-Hill Book Co., 1960.

Crook, William H. *Memories of the White House: The Home Life of Our Presidents from Lincoln to Roosevelt*. Boston: Little, Brown and Co., 1911.

Depew, Chauncey M. *My Memories of Eighty Years*. New York: Charles Scribner's Sons, 1922.

"Frances Folsom Cleveland." *History of Buffalo*. <http://ah.bfn.org/h/cleve/ffc/>.

"Frances Folsom Cleveland—Legacy." <http://www.politicalquest.org/index. php/cssID/479/csf/Frances_Folsom_Cleveland.html>.

Gilder, Richard Watson. *Grover Cleveland: A Record of Friendship*. New York: Century Company, 1910.

Gilder, Rosamond, ed. *Letters of Richard Watson Gilder*. Boston: Houghton Mifflin Co., 1916.

Gwynn, Stephen. 1929. *The Letters and Friendships of Sir Cecil Spring-Rice, A Record*. Vol. 1. Boston: Houghton Mifflin Co., 1929.

Hoover, Irwin (Ike) Hood. 1934. *Forty-two Years in the White House*. Boston: Houghton Mifflin Co., 1934.

John, Arthur. 1981. *The Best Years of the Century: Richard Watson Gilder, "Scribner's Monthly," and the "Century Magazine," 1870-1909*. Urbana: University of Illinois Press, 1981.

Keim, DeB. Randolph. *Handbook of Official and Social Etiquette and Public Ceremonials at Washington*. 3rd ed. Washington, D.C: De B. Randolph Keim, 1889.

Jeffries, Ona Griffin. *In and Out of the White House*. New York: Wilfred Funk, Inc., 1960.

MacArthur, Burke. *United Littles: The Story of the Needlework Guild of America*. New York: Coward-McCann, Inc., 1955.

McElroy, Robert. *Grover Cleveland: The Man and the Statesman*. Vol. 1. New York: Harper & Bros., 1923.

———. "Patriotism—Past Present and Future." In *Proceedings and Addresses*, 94–96. Washington, DC: National Education Association, 1918.

Merrill, Horace. Bourbon Leader: Grover Cleveland and the Democratic Party. Boston: Little, Brown & Co., 1957.

National Security League. "The Flying Squadron of Speakers: A Propaganda Regiment for Patriotic Service." New York: National Security League, 1919.

Nevins, Alan. *Grover Cleveland: Portrait of Courage*. New York: Dodd, Mead & Co., 1932.

———, ed. *Letters of Grover Cleveland, 1850–1908*. Boston: Houghton Mifflin, Co., 1933.

Parker, George F. *Recollections of Grover Cleveland*. New York: Century Co., 1909.

"Pedigree of Stephen Grover Cleveland." <http://www.concentric.net/~pvb/ GEN/presclev.html>.

Pendleton, Leila Amos. "A Narrative of the Negro." <http://docsouth.unc. edu/pendleton/pendle.htm>.

Perling, J. J. *Presidents' Sons*. New York: Odyssey Press, 1947.

"(Preston) Cleveland, Frances Folsom." <http://www.firstladies.org/Bibliography/ FrancesCleveland>.

Ross, Elizabeth Dale. *The Kindergarten Crusade: The Establishment of Preschool Education in the United States*. Athens: Ohio University Press, 1976.

Sadler, Christine. *Children in the White House*. New York: G. P. Putnam's Sons, 1967.

Severn, Sue. "Frances Folsom Cleveland." In *American First Ladies: Their Lives and Legacy*, ed. Lewis Gould, 243–59. New York: Garland Publishing, 1996.

Sims, J. F. "Patriotism in the Schools." In *Proceedings and Addresses*, 169–70. Washington, DC: National Education Association, 1917.

Strouse, Jean. *Morgan: American Financier*. New York: Random House, 1999.

Topalian, Naomi. *A Legacy of Honor*. Watertown, MA: Baikar Publishing, 1995.

Truman, Margaret. *First Ladies*. New York: Random House, 1995.

Tugwell, Rexford G. *Grover Cleveland*. New York: Macmillan Co., 1968.

Tyrrell, Ian. *Woman's World; Woman's Empire*. Chapel Hill: University of North Carolina Press, 1991.

Wheeler, George. *Pierpont Morgan and Friends: The Anatomy of a Myth*. Englewood Cliffs, NJ: Prentice-Hall, 1973.

Williams, Francis Howard. *The Bride of the White House*. Philadelphia: Bradley & Co., 1886.

## COLLECTIONS

Frances Folsom Cleveland Papers. Louis Jefferson Long Library, Wells College, Aurora, NY.

Grover Cleveland Birthplace Museum. Caldwell, NJ.

Grover Cleveland Papers. Library of Congress.

Helena Gilder Papers, Lilly Library, Indiana University, Bloomington, IN.

Theodore Roosevelt Papers. Library of Congress.

Virginia Waller Johnson Papers, Virginia Historical Society, Richmond, VA.

## PERIODICALS

*Atlantic Monthly*
*Century Magazine*
*Collier's*
*Cosmopolitan*
*Critic*

*Harper's Bazaar*
*Harper's Weekly*
*Ladies' Home Journal*
*McClure's Magazine*
*PTA Magazine*
*Public Opinion*
*Saturday Evening Post*

## NEWSPAPERS

*Baltimore Sun*
*Boston Globe*
*New York Times*
*Washington Post*

# Index